THE AMERICAN CONSTITUTIONAL SYSTEM UNDER STRONG AND WEAK PARTIES

THE AMERICAN CONSTITUTIONAL SYSTEM UNDER STRONG AND WEAK PARTIES

Edited by
Patricia Bonomi
James MacGregor Burns
Austin Ranney

For Project '87, sponsored jointly by
the American Historical Association
and the American Political Science Association

PRAEGER

PRAEGER SPECIAL STUDIES • PRAEGER SCIENTIFIC

Library of Congress Cataloging in Publication Data

Main entry under title:

The American constitutional system under strong
   and weak parties.

   1. Political parties--United States--History--
Addresses, essays, lectures. I. Bonomi, Patricia
U. II. Burns, James MacGregor. III. Ranney,
Austin, IV. American Historical Association.
V. American Political Science Association.
JK2261.A5   324.273'o9   80-39659
ISBN 0-03-059041-8

Published in 1981 by Praeger Publishers
CBS Educational and Professional Publishing
A Division of CBS, Inc.
521 Fifth Avenue, New York, New York 10175 U.S.A.

123456789   145   987654321

Printed in the United States of America

CONTENTS

LIST OF DISCUSSANTS

RICHARD M. ABRAMS, University of California, Berkeley
JAMES M. BANNER, JR., Princeton University
LEE BENSON, University of Pennsylvania
PATRICIA BONOMI, New York University
JAMES MacGREGOR BURNS, Williams College
NOBLE E. CUNNINGHAM, JR., University of Missouri, Columbia
RONALD P. FORMISANO, Clark University
DONALD M. FRASER, Mayor of Minneapolis, Minnesota
FRANK FREIDEL, Harvard University
OTIS L. GRAHAM, University of California, Santa Barbara
KERMIT HALL, Wayne State University
JUDSON L. JAMES, Virginia Polytechnic Institute and State University
WILLIAM J. KEEFE, University of Pittsburgh
LINDA K. KERBER, University of Iowa
EVERETT CARLL LADD, JR., University of Connecticut
KAY LAWSON, San Francisco State University
ARTHUR S. LINK, Princeton University
ROBERT McCLORY, U.S. Representative from Illinois
RICHARD P. McCORMICK, Rutgers University
RICHARD B. MORRIS, Columbia University
GERALD M. POMPER, Rutgers University
AUSTIN RANNEY, American Enterprise Institute for Public Policy Research
DONALD A. ROBINSON, Smith College
ARTHUR M. SCHLESINGER, JR., City University of New York
JAMES L. SUNDQUIST, Brookings Institution
DAVID P. THELEN, University of Missouri, Columbia

INTRODUCTION

This volume stems from a conference sponsored by Project '87, a program conducted jointly by the American Historical Association and the American Political Science Association to celebrate the bicentennial of the U.S. Constitution by improving and disseminating knowledge about the Constitution and the political and governmental system that has grown up around it.

The conference, organized by the coeditors, was held at Williamsburg, Virginia, on April 27 and 28, 1979. There were four sessions, each focusing upon one of the papers that constitute the chapters of this volume. The discussions were recorded and transcribed, and edited selections from each session appear at the end of each chapter. The names and affiliations of the discussants are listed immediately following the table of contents.

The conference and this volume both take their departure from the fact that in recent years, and particularly since 1968, U.S. political parties have undergone one of the most sweeping series of changes in their histories.[1] Some of these changes have resulted from changes in the parties' own rules. Both parties, but particularly the Democrats, have radically altered the rules by which they choose their national convention delegates, and the Supreme Court has held that the national party rules have higher legal status than the primary law of any state that may conflict with them.[2] The Democrats have adopted the first major party national charter, and, in 1974 and 1978, held the first major party midterm conferences in our history.

Other changes have resulted from changes in state laws, notably in the proliferation of presidential primaries. In 1968 only 16 states and the District of Columbia held presidential primaries, and only 37 percent of the delegates to the Democratic national convention and 34 percent of Republican delegates were chosen or bound by primaries. In 1976, 29 states and D.C. held presidential primaries, and the proportions of delegates chosen or bound by them soared to 73 percent and 68 percent respectively. The highest tide yet came in 1980, when 35 states, D.C., and Puerto Rico held presidential primaries and the proportions of delegates so chosen or bound approached 80 percent in both parties. And in 1974, Congress for the first time in our history adopted public funding not only for the general election campaigning of the two major parties' presidential candidates but also for the preconvention campaigning of both parties' aspirants for the nominations.

Still other changes have taken place in public esteem for the parties. Surveys by the University of Michigan's Center for Political studies show that in 1964, 76 percent of U.S. adults identified to some degree with either the Democratic or Republican parties, but in 1976 the proportion of identifiers had fallen to 63 percent. Another change is that the proportion of voters voting straight party tickets has fallen from 65 percent in 1960 to 33 percent in 1976. Still another is the 1976 Gallup poll finding that 68 percent of U.S. citizens believe that presidential candidates should be chosen by national primaries, rather than by national party conventions.[3]

There is no little disagreement among political scientists, historians, politicians, and other party watchers about what all of these changes mean for the state of the parties and the health of the polity. Some commentators think that the parties are much the better for it — that their decision-making processes are more open, more participatory, and more fair than they have ever been; some add that all we need to do now is to extend public financing to congressional elections and make sure that at least half of all national convention delegates are women.[4] Others believe that the net effect of these changes has been what Jeane Kirkpatrick calls "the dismantling of the parties," with the result, intended or not, that they now play no significant role in the vetting of presidential aspirants; in the selection of nominees; in the organization, financing, and conduct of presidential campaigns; or, indeed, in any of the activities in which they were once the sole or main agencies.[5]

But while the commentators have debated the questions of whether the parties are better or worse, stronger or weaker, than before 1968, few have explicitly faced other, but at least equally important, questions: *What difference does it make?* Have U.S. parties ever been truly strong? If so, in what respects were they strong? What made them strong? What role did their strength enable them to play in the larger political system? What values were served and what values were damaged by that role?

This book is grounded in the belief that answers to these questions will help us to decide whether the parties of the 1980s are especially strong or weak and to calculate what the consequences are likely to be for the U.S. constitutional system. We believe that the book's papers and discussions by a distinguished group of historians, political scientists, and party practitioners can contribute significantly to our understanding of the questions and, therefore, of the state of our constitutional system as it enters its third century.

The Editors

NOTES

1. The changes listed in the text are described in greater detail in Austin Ranney, "The Political Parties: Reform and Decline," in *The New American Political System,* ed. Anthony King (Washington, D.C.: American Enterprise Institute for Public Policy Research, 1978), pp. 213-47.

2. *Cousins v. Wigoda,* 419 U.S. 477 (1975).

3. Gallup Poll, release of February 26, 1976.

4. The leading expositions of this view are William J. Crotty, *Political Reform and the American Experiment* (New York: Thomas Y. Crowell, 1977); and Crotty, *Decision for the Democrats: Reforming the Party Structure* (Baltimore, Md.: Johns Hopkins University Press, 1978).

5. For expressions of this view, see Walter Dean Burnham, "The End of American Party Politics," *Trans-action* (December 1969); Jeane Jordan Kirkpatrick, *Dismantling the Parties* (Washington, D.C.: American Enterprise Institute for Public Policy Research, 1978); David S. Broder, *The Party's Over* (New York: Harper & Row, 1972); and Everett Carll Ladd, Jr., *Where Have All the Voters Gone?* (New York: Norton, 1978).

THE AMERICAN CONSTITUTIONAL SYSTEM UNDER STRONG AND WEAK PARTIES

PRESIDENTIAL LEADERSHIP, POLITICAL PARTIES, AND THE CONGRESSIONAL CAUCUS, 1800-1824

Noble E. Cunningham, Jr.

The quarter century that opened with Thomas Jefferson's victory in the election of 1800 and closed with the breakup of the Republican party in 1824 offers useful insights into the role of strong and weak parties in the United States. Although the operation of the congressional nominating caucus lends a certain unity to the political history of the era, the contrasts between Jefferson's presidency at the beginning of the period and James Monroe's administration at the end of the era were considerable. During Monroe's first term, John Quincy Adams criticized the caucus as "a practice which places the President in a state of undue subserviency to the members of the legislature."[1] Such a criticism, would not have been applicable to Jefferson's presidency, for the political systems under Jefferson and Monroe were far different than these presidents' party identities as Republicans might suggest. Important keys to understanding these differences may be found in the role of presidential leadership and the changing state of national political parties.

The first congressional caucuses to decide either presidential or vice-presidential nominations met in May 1800, when Federalist and Republican members of Congress caucused separately. In the only instance when the Federalists employed that device, the Federalist caucus agreed to support John Adams and Charles C. Pinckney equally as candidates. The Republican caucus, the first in a series through 1824, decided to support Aaron Burr as vice-president on the ticket with Jefferson, whom a Republican consensus had already designated the Republican candidate for president. It is significant that Jefferson did not owe his nomination to the Republican caucus, although he clearly had

1

the overwhelming endorsement of that body. Four years later, the Republican nominating caucus — now formal and publicly reported, in contrast to the secretive meeting of 1800 — placed Jefferson's name in nomination for a second term.[2] This was unnecessary, for Jefferson's popular support was even broader in 1804 than in 1800; but the action demonstrated that the Republican caucus had assumed the critical function of nominating presidential and vice-presidential candidates. The caucus provided even greater proof of its powerful role by dropping the incumbent vice-president, Aaron Burr, from the party ticket and nominating George Clinton to succeed him. The caucus had thus positioned itself to decide the even more difficult question of who was to be supported as Jefferson's successor at the end of his second term; in 1808, the caucus made that decision. Jefferson's successors during the period of the ascendance of the caucus, therefore, were to have a different relationship to the caucus than Jefferson had, which explains much about the political relationships that underlay the presidencies of Madison and Monroe.

JEFFERSON LEADS THE PARTY

Although Jefferson owed no direct debt to the Republican caucus, what the caucus represented was important both to his election and to the conduct of his presidency because the Republican caucus symbolized the importance of party in Congress. Efforts to denigrate the role of parties under Jefferson by comparing their characteristics and functions with more modern political parties are not helpful to a historical understanding of the period. The election of 1800 was as clear a party contest as any election in U.S. history, and party was a major factor in the process of government under Jefferson. When the tie in the electoral vote between Jefferson and Burr in 1800 went to the House of Representatives, party was paramount. Not a single Republican member deserted Jefferson to vote for Burr, and no Federalist-controlled state ever voted for Jefferson, although Federalists finally permitted Jefferson's election by not voting or by casting blank ballots. With the adoption of the Twelfth Amendment in 1804, strong parties produced the first major alteration in the electoral mechanism specified by the Constitution.

The victory of the Republican party in 1800 was more impressive in the congressional elections than in the narrow Republican victory in the electoral college. In the new Congress that assembled in 1801, the Republicans had a commanding majority[3] and they proceeded to reorganize Congress along party lines. Nathaniel Macon, a staunch Republican, was elected Speaker of the House, and John Beckley, one of the most ardent party workers and active campaign managers in the country, was restored to the clerkship of the House, from which he had been removed after the Federalist victory in 1796. The new Republican Speaker, in whose hands resided the power to appoint all standing committees, named Republican majorities to all these committees. In the Senate, where every committee was elected by ballot, Republicans had majorities on 76 percent of all committees elected during the first session of the Seventh Congress, and seven out of the eight leading Senators, in terms of committee service, were Republicans. By the Tenth Congress, Republicans controlled 94 percent of all Senate committees. Throughout the period of Jefferson's presidency, the Federalist and Republican parties won votes for Senate committees that were roughly proportionate to their respective party strengths in that body.[4]

Outside of Congress, in the boardinghouse of Washington, members segregated themselves by party. Although sectional associations were evident in the boardinghouse groups, whenever sectional attachment and party affiliation conflicted, party invariably prevailed. Most houses contained a majority from one section of the country and a few were exclusively sectional, but all were rigidly partisan in composition. At the first session of the Seventh Congress, convening in December 1801, of 11 boardinghouse groups of from six to twelve members each, 7 were Republican and 4 were Federalist; not one contained members of opposite parties. The separation by parties was almost as pronounced at the end of Jefferson's presidency as at the beginning. In 1807, there were only two Federalist boardinghouses, but most of the 28 Federalists in Congress lived in one of these two houses, and only 3 Federalists boarded with Republicans.[5] To dismiss party identification as being unimportant because members were not identified by party in congressional rosters is to miss one of the most pervasive influences on the conduct of the members of the national legislature.[6]

In organizing the executive branch, Jefferson was as partisan as the Republicans in Congress. He named only Republicans to his cabinet and to the principal offices under his appointment. Although he left about half of all Federalist federal officeholders in their jobs, and in so doing demonstrated more moderation than many of his ardent supporters felt was justified, he affirmed that until Republicans had their proportionate share of federal offices, party affiliation must be considered in making appointments. Jefferson doubtless was sincere in his desire to reconcile parties when he declared in his inaugural address that "we are all republicans: we are all federalists," but what he had in mind was that all Federalists become Republicans. When this did not take place, he dismissed as unworthy of serious consideration those Federalists whom he was unable to convert. In practice, he never recognized the legitimacy of the Federalist opposition.

Jefferson was the first president to accept the dual responsiblity of being the head of the nation and the head of a political party. He commanded the loyalty of Republicans throughout the country and, even when the party became divided in local disputes, he retained the allegiance of nearly all. As president, Jefferson enjoyed a broad base of popular support that gave him powerful leverage with Congress and a strength of leadership that neither Madison nor Monroe was to enjoy.

In his relations with Congress, Jefferson exerted a strong leadership role. In his annual messages and special messages he recommended the major legislative program that Congress enacted, and by working directly to get his legislative program adopted he went far beyond the making of recommendations. He drafted bills and sent them to friendly members in Congress to be introduced. He used members of his cabinet to convey other proposals and suggestions to congressional committees and individual members. While Congress was in session, Jefferson invited small groups of members for dinner at the executive mansion three nights each week throughout the session. The most frequent invitations went to leading members.

With only partial success, Jefferson attempted to develop on the floor of the House of Representatives an administrative spokesman who would actively work to advance the measures of the administration, or, in Jefferson's words, "not suffer them to go off in sleep, but bring them to the attention of the house and give them a fair chance."[7] Jefferson tried to maintain such a relationship with John Randolph of Roanoke, chairman of the House Committee of Ways and Means. For a time, Randolph assumed the role of a floor leader in the House, but he remained independent of presidential direction and in 1806 broke with the president. Although Randolph had come to his position of leadership through the mechanisms of the House, not the influence of the president, he was unable to maintain that leadership once he broke with Jefferson. In 1807, the Republican majority in the House refused to reelect Randolph's old friend Nathaniel Macon as Speaker, and under the new Speaker, Joseph B. Varnum, Randolph lost his chairmanship of the Committee of Ways and Means. Thus was it demonstrated that supporting of the administration was essential to retaining a Republican leadership role in Congress under Jefferson.

As president, Jefferson maintained contact with Republican party leaders both in Congress and in the states. On trips to their home states, members of his administration collected political intelligence for the president, and some members of Congress reported to him by letter on public opinion in their districts when they returned home. Jefferson also used his dinner parties to collect information on public sentiment throughout the country. He watched with interest, and encouraged in every way he could, the growth of the Republican party in New England. He worried about party divisions in older Republican states and made pleas for party unity, although he never intervened in local party schisms. The mechanisms of the Republican party furnished Jefferson a means of staying in touch with a national constituency and, since he regarded the Republican party as representing the great majority of the citizens, a means of learning public opinion.

The cohesiveness of the Republican party both within Congress and in the country was directly related to the strength or weakness of the Federalist opposition. Only in the first of the four Congresses that met under Jefferson were Federalists strong enough to be an effective opposition. By the beginning of Jefferson's second term, Federalists in the House numbered 27 out of 142: "not quite one 5th of the house − not a sufficient number to demand the yeas and nays to be entered on the journals," one Federalist pointed out.[8]

In 1806, John Randolph's defection threatened to divide congressional Republicans, but Randolph carried into opposition only a small group of five or six disaffected Republicans. Jefferson, who had taken steps to isolate Randolph, believed that the alarm created by Randolph's revolt "produced a rallying together and a harmony, which carelessness and security had begun to endanger."[9] Even in times of declining Federalist strength, the fear of a Federalist revival also served as a check on Republican divisions, for Republicans in Jefferson's day did not know that the Federalists would never return to power in the national government.

Jefferson's relations with Congress were aided by the collegiality and the stability of his cabinet and by no member of his administration's attempting to build independent support in Congress. Although there was some friction in the cabinet between Secretary of the Treasury Albert Gallatin and Secretary of the Navy Robert Smith, their differences were reconciled in the cabinet or decided by the president and were never carried to Congress. Jefferson looked back on his presidency as "an example of harmony in a cabinet of six persons, to which perhaps history has furnished no parallel."[10] In a similar vein, John Quincy Adams observed at the beginning of Monroe's presidency in 1817 that "Mr. Jefferson alone of our four Presidents has had the good fortune of a Cabinet, harmonizing with each other, and with him through the whole of his Administration."[11]

The influence of the executive branch on the legislative process was promoted by Congress's lack of staff services. Neither Congressmen nor congressional committees had staffs; indeed, members did not even have offices. Thus, the legislature was highly dependent upon the executive departments to provide information necessary to the legislative process. The first action of a congressional committee commonly was to request information from a department office and not infrequently also to ask the department head for recommendations. Reports from department heads were often incorporated into committee reports; committee chairmen regularly consulted with department officers, and sometimes they even called for the assistance of department clerks.

Jefferson never exerted the control over Congress seen by his Federalist critics, who charged that "the President has only to act and the Majority will approve,"[12] and that Jefferson *"behind the curtain,* directs the measures he wishes to have adopted; while in each house a majority of puppets move as he touches the wires."[13] But there is ample proof that Jefferson provided strong presidential direction.[14]

A strong Republican party was a key factor in the success of Jefferson's leadership. The strength and loyalty of his party in Congress gave him great support there and made the Republican party an effective channel of cooperation between the president and the Congress. Jefferson's role as the head of the party gave him a leverage and bargaining power with Congress that no previous president had enjoyed. Under presidential leadership, party provided the majority in Congress a sense of direction, the guidelines for a legislative program, and an impetus for making legislative decisions. The argument that once in power the Republicans deserted their out-of-power views has been exaggerated. The Republicans in Congress carried out their campaign promises to reduce the army, the navy, government expenditures, and the size of the government establishment. They began paying off the national debt, lowered naturalization requirements, and managed without alien and sedition laws. By carrying out policies that they had advocated in seeking power, the Republicans demonstrated the role that party could play in the formation of public policy. Although the Republican party was so strong in numbers in the Jeffersonian Congresses that internal divisions developed, these were never strong enough to destroy the basic cohesiveness of the majority in Congress as long as Jefferson remained in office. Under Jefferson, then, a strong national party contributed to strong presidential leadership. As impressive as were Jefferson's own leadership skills, without a strong party his effectiveness as president could only have been lessened.

THE PARTY LEADS MADISON

Although Jefferson clearly favored Madison as his successor, the Republican congressional caucus that met in 1808 did not assemble simply to confirm the President's choice. Until the caucus made its decision, it was not clear who the Republican candidate would be. New York members were working hard to gather support for Vice-President George Clinton. John Randolph was openly supporting James Monroe; and Monroe's strength in Virginia, the nation's largest state, extended far beyond Randolph's followers. In fact, there was an active movement among Monroe's supporters in Virginia to challenge the congressional caucus. One Virginia Republican leader, in December 1807, predicted that Monroe would be placed in nomination by the Virginia assembly. "They seem to be opposed to a *caucus* at Washington fixing a President and Vice President upon the States," he observed.[15] Indeed, the movement for Monroe in Virginia was gaining such strength that Madison's backers there began appealing to Virginia friends in Congress to convene an early meeting of the congressional caucus in Washington to nominate Madison so Monroe's supporters in Virginia would be undermined. "Confident in their supposed strength in this State, they talk of bringing forward Col. Monroe, at once, without waiting for the meeting in Washington," an alarmed Governor William H. Cabell wrote to Senator Wilson Cary Nicholas early in January 1808. "I hope therefore you will soon have a meeting at Congress, and ascertain, in a way which cannot be mistaken, the sentiments of the other republican States."[16]

The convening of the congressional caucus in Washington on January 23, 1808, came at the instigation of Virginia Madisonians in Congress, who, convinced that Madison had a majority there, were anxious to head off the Monroe movement in Virginia. As a consequence, the caucus was boycotted by the supporters of Monroe as well as by the friends of Clinton. "It was a pretty general understanding among those who did not wish to support Madison not to attend the meeting," one Congressman reported.[17] Nevertheless, a majority of the Republican membership of the two houses of Congress did attend, and Madison received 83 of the 89 votes cast in the caucus — a solid majority of the Republicans in Congress.[18]

What is most important to recognize in regard to the caucus of 1808 is that it made a real decision. Before the caucus met, there was no clear Republican consensus. The caucus was crucial in establishing Madison as the Republican nominee for president. "You may rely on it his election was a very up hill business 'till the republican members of Congress give the vote in his favor," a Pennsylvania Republican confided to Jefferson. "Many is the time I have heard the cry Clinton was the man he would sweep from office all the old Tories and federalists."[19] Unlike Jefferson, Madison did not have the unanimous support of Republicans throughout the country; the caucus nomination was essential to consolidate party support behind him. There were clearly constraints imposed on the caucus by state and local party sentiment with which members of Congress were in touch, but the caucus did more than confirm a recognized party consensus.

The caucus decision in 1808 and Madison's subsequent election not only established more firmly than ever the power of the caucus to control the party's nominations for president and vice-president, but also created a relationship between the president and the caucus that had not existed before — one that forecast the rising power of Congress and a decline of presidential leadership.

Madison's victory in 1808 was decisive enough. He won 122 electoral votes to Federalist Charles C. Pinckney's 47. But Pinckney had received only 14 electoral votes running against Jefferson in 1804, and his vote in 1808 was evidence of the Federalist revival stimulated by the unpopular embargo of 1807. Also important was that some New York Republicans refused to give up George Clinton after the caucus nominated Madison, and Clinton received 6 of New York's 19 electoral votes for president in 1808, while being elected vice-president.

Unlike Jefferson, Madison did not begin his presidency as the recognized head of the Republican party. In 1808, he had not played the kind of active role in rallying his party and advancing his own election that Jefferson had done in 1800, but in preelection maneuvering he had been solicitous of Congressmen who controlled the party's nomination. "Mr. Madison . . . gives dinners and makes generous displays to the Members," Senator Samuel L. Mitchill observed as the election year 1808 approached, adding also that "the Secretary of State has a wife to aid his pretensions. . . . And in these two Respects Mr. Madison is going greatly ahead of [Clinton] ."[20] Madison built his support more in Congress than in the country at large although, as the election showed, he had substantial popular strength. But he did not have the ties to state party leaders that Jefferson had enjoyed. Obligated to the congressional caucus for his nomination, Madison was dependent on the support of his party in Congress in a way that Jefferson had never been.

The reality of his new relationship became immediately apparent when Madison took office. Congress did not even allow the new president to form his own cabinet without interference. When Madison proposed to nominate Albert Gallatin as secretary of state, he met powerful resistance from a group of Republican senators who threatened to block Gallatin's confirmation in the Senate. As a consequence, Madison kept Gallatin at the head of the Treasury Department, where he needed no Senate approval to remain, and gave the critical post of secretary of state to Robert Smith, whose brother, Samuel Smith, was one of the leaders of the anti-Gallatin faction in the Senate.[21] It was an inauspicious beginning to an administration that was to be plagued by Republican factionalism in Congress, instability in the cabinet, and ineffectiveness in leadership.

Madison never recovered the leadership power that he let slip from his hands. After two years, he dismissed Robert Smith and brought James Monroe into his Cabinet, but congressional opponents forced Gallatin out of the administration. His difficulties with Congress were evident in his use of the veto. In vetoing seven measures, Madison vetoed more acts than had all the three presidents before him.[22] Madison's relations with Congress coincided with the principles of checks and balances in which he so firmly believed, but the record of his presidency was weak in legislative accomplishments and administrative achievements. For the war years, the Madisonian system was nearly disastrous.

Jefferson had complained about the slowness of Congress to act, about the lack of "men of business" to keep his legislative program moving, and about Republicans who acted too independently of party. With more reason, Madison also complained about Congress. "Congress remain in the unhinged state which has latterly marked their proceedings," he wrote to Jefferson in 1810. A majority in the House had "stuck together" to pass one important measure, but "what the Senate will do with the Bill is rendered utterly uncertain by the policy which seems to prevail in that branch."[23] When Jefferson had complained, he also had tried to do something about the situation by encouraging certain members to assume leadership roles in Congress, urging capable men to run for Congress, and at times using his own considerable influence to defuse situations that seriously threatened to disrupt Republican party unity. The best example of this was Jefferson's success in isolating Randolph after his break with the administration. Madison, however, only complained, concluded with resignation that he was powerless to alter the course of Congress, and accepted his difficulties as the consequences of republican government.

Had Madison chosen to follow Jefferson's model of presidential leadership, he would have found in many parts of the country strong loyalty to the

Republican party, clear party identity, and well-organized state and local party machinery. That party was still important was demonstrated in the most important decision of Madison's presidency: the decision for war in 1812. Recent studies of the War of 1812 have shown that in the vote on the declaration of war, party provides the most satisfactory explanation for the decision.[24] The election of 1812 also demonstrated that parties were still very much alive. Norman Risjord has written that "in an organizational sense the election of 1812 was the pinacle of the first party system."[25] It was also the closest election between 1800 and 1824, the result of both the revival of Federalist strength and the candidacy of DeWitt Clinton, who challenged the Republican congressional caucus nomination of Madison. A shift of 20 of the 217 electoral votes from Madison to Clinton would have made Clinton president. Both Madison and the caucus survived Clinton's challenge, but both were weakened by it, leaving political power even more splintered.

Except in 1800 and 1804, the caucus decision had not gone unchallenged, and as an agency for making presidential and vice-presidential nominations it had never become fully accepted. Each time the caucus met, there was a debate over whether members of Congress could properly act in a nominating capacity. Although there was ground for argument over the constitutional principles of separation of powers — and these principles were always stressed — defending or denouncing the caucus most commonly depended upon whether the caucus supported the nominee of one's choice. As long as the caucus continued to make recommendations, it was still to a candidate's advantage to have its support. As election year 1816 approached, the caucus decision again appeared important. Supporters of both Secretary of State Monroe, the administration's heir-apparent, and of Secretary of the Treasury William H. Crawford, who enjoyed considerable support in Congress, recognized this. Monroe's backers preferred no caucus at all to one that they were unsure of controlling. In fact, they saw the opposing forces as so evenly matched and the outcome of a caucus as so uncertain that they seriously considered not employing the caucus and allowing their candidate to be nominated by state legislatures.[26]

On March 10, 1816, an unsigned, printed notice addressed to the Republican members of Congress was circulated, calling a meeting of the caucus to nominate presidential and vice-presidential candidates on March 12.[27] It was suspected, and events later confirmed, that this caucus was called by the friends of Crawford. When less than a majority of Republicans attended, the caucus confined itself to issuing a call for a full caucus on March 16. Monroe's friends had little choice but to be present at the second meeting, which was well attended, and the vote was close: 65 for Monroe and 54 for Crawford.[28] Monroe's biographer, Harry Ammon, believes that Monroe won because he was popular with state party leaders. Monroe had been endorsed by Republican state conventions in Rhode Island and Massachusetts and by the legislature of Pennsylvania. Congressmen, whatever their personal preferences, could not afford to ignore such endorsements.[29]

It would appear, then, that Monroe had a base of support in the states upon which he might have built and reasserted presidential leadership on the model set by Jefferson. But this was not to be, for the state of parties was vastly different in 1816 from what it had been in 1800, and Monroe's own attitude toward political parties differed significantly from that of Jefferson. The major contest in the election of 1816 turned out to be that in Congress over the caucus nomination. The Federalists were so discredited by their opposition to the War of 1812 and by the Hartford Convention that the shattered party made no formal nomination. Rufus King, tacitly the Federalist candidate, carried only three states and won 34 electoral votes to Monroe's 16 states and 183 electoral votes. The collapse of the Federalist party fitted neatly into Monroe's views on parties. So also would the decline of the Republican party that was already beginning.

THE MONROE ADMINISTRATION:
DECLINE OF PARTY INFLUENCE

Madison believed that political parties were evils that were unavoidable in free states; Monroe believed that parties were evils that could be prevented or abolished.[30] Many men "are of the opinion that the existence of the federal party is necessary to keep union and order in the republican ranks, that is that free government cannot exist without parties," he wrote soon after his election to the presidency in 1816. "This is not my opinion."[31] Monroe sought, therefore, to "exterminate all party divisions in our country"[32] and he affirmed that "the Chief Magistrate of the Country ought not be the head of a party, but of the nation itself."[33] The decline of parties that Monroe applauded and sought to promote was indeed real. There may never have been an "era of good feelings", but under Monroe the country experienced a period when parties were the weakest they had ever been since their formation in the early 1790s.

On the day that Monroe was inaugurated as president, one member of Congress, reviewing the session that had just closed, in a letter to his constituents noted that "party spirit is so far extinct, that the time seems to have passed away, and I fondly hope will never again occur, when party measures . . . can be carried by the mere force of a name."[34] Another member reporting on the same session agreed that "among the most auspicious appearances of the times, is the obliteration of party spirit. No question at the present session of congress has been discussed or determined on the ground of party."[35]

Many Republicans and a few Federalists still identified themselves with parties, but numerous new members entered Congress without party labels. There were 126 new members among the 185 representatives in the House of Representatives that assembled at the beginning of Monroe's administration,[36] and party was less important in the legislative branch than it had been since the

Republican opposition had formed around Madison in the Second Congress. "Nothing like the present state of things has been experienced since the adoption of the Constitution," wrote New Hampshire's Jeremiah Mason after resigning from the Senate in 1817. "For the last sixteen years (I think I may say twenty) the government has been carried on by party spirit. What is now to be substituted?"[37] The decline of parties in Congress was accompanied by a decline of parties on the state level. Republican party organization, discipline, and activity declined in such once highly organized and warmly partisan states as Pennsylvania, New Jersey, and Massachusetts.[38] The weakness of parties in the period of Monroe's presidency is the key to the declining influence of presidential leadership and the rising power of Congress. "The Executive has no longer a commanding influence," Justice Joseph Story observed in 1818. "The House of Representatives has absorbed all the popular feeling and all the effective power of the country."[39]

The major mechanisms for wielding congressional power – the Speakership and congressional committees – that were to be employed under Monroe were not innovations. Their powers had been demonstrated under Jefferson. In 1806, Congressman Barnabas Bidewell observed:

> In every legislature, the introduction, progress, and conclusion of business depend much upon committees; and, in the House of Representatives of the U.S., more than in any other legislative body within my knowledge, the business referred to Committees, and reported on by them, is, by usage and common consent, controlled by their chairman. As the Speaker, according to the standing rules of the House, has the appointment of Committees, he has it in his power to place whom he pleases in the foreground, and whom he please in the background, and thus, in some measure, affect their agency in the transactions of the House.[40]

But under Jefferson, party supplied a common bond between the president, department heads, and Republican committee chairman. Thus, in 1801, when a committee was appointed to investigate the Treasury Department, Secretary of the Treasury Albert Gallatin supplied the committee chairman with the list of questions that the committee would ask the Secretary of the Treasury, and he went over the committees's final report with the chairman.[41] Such a party bond did not exist under Monroe.

Although the Speaker of the House had no more power under Monroe than under Jefferson, he exercised his power more independently and exerted more initiative in the legislative process. Nathaniel Macon had lost the Speakership in 1807 because of the paucity of his support of the president; Speaker Henry Clay increased his influence by opposing President Monroe and pushing his own program in Congress. He also maintained his position by distributing committee appointments among various factions and not excluding supporters of rival candidates for the presidency.[42]

There were more standing committees in Congress during Monroe's administration than there were during Jefferson's. In 1816, the Senate, for the first time, created a system of standing committees similar to that of the House, where the committee system had been evolving since the 1790s. At about the same time, the House expanded its committee structure by adding six new committees on expenditures to oversee each of the departments and the expenditures for public buildings.[43] More important than the creation of new committees was their more vigorous oversight over department offices, their broadening use of investigative power,[44] and their more active role in the initiation of legislation.

The differences in the role of the Speaker and of committees under Jefferson and Monroe are not alone sufficient to explain the weakness of presidential leadership under Monroe. The weakness of party and Monroe's refusal to be the leader of a party were fundamental to his dearth of influence. A decline of a sense of party led to a decline of cooperation based on party between the president and his party in Congress. Under Jefferson, the Republican party had provided the president with a national power base and had served as a channel of cooperation between him and the Congress. In abdicating the role of party leader, Monroe threw away much of the bargaining power that a party leader like Jefferson had been able to use. The decline of the nationally organized Republican party also led to the rise of sectional groupings and to sectional, rather than party, positions on such issues as the tariff and internal improvements. The decline of parties also produced personal followings such as had characterized the preparty conditions of the early 1790s. William H. Crawford, Henry Clay, John Quincy Adams, John C. Calhoun, and Andrew Jackson all had their followings or were trying to build them. Since Crawford, Adams, and Calhoun were all in Monroe's cabinet, holding the three principal cabinet posts of Treasury, State, and War, the cabinet under Monroe was obviously a different mechanism than it had been under Jefferson. The decline of party in which Monroe so much gloried transformed the operation of the executive more fundamentally than he realized.[45]

The cabinet system under Monroe became essentially one in which the leading members of the cabinet were nearly independent ministers, each with a bloc of supporters in Congress, and policy decisions were made by finding positions that could command the support of these political leaders and their followers in Congress — and also their constituencies outside Congress. Within certain limits, Monroe made the system work. The cabinet met more regularly and more frequently than ever before. We know a great deal about these innumerable cabinet meetings from the extensive reports in Adams's diary, and it is clear that many long cabinet meetings were used to hammer out agreements, harmonize conflicting opinions, and secure the commitments of cabinet members to specific policies and programs. Once the cabinet had agreed upon measures, the prospects of getting them through Congress were promising, and Monroe's record in this respect was good.[46] But Monroe paid a price in executive leadership. He avoided subjects on which he knew there were irreconcilable differences among the members of his cabinet, and he refrained from making recommendations to Congress on issues that could not command cabinet agreement. On the controversy over the admission of Missouri — one of the most critical questions of his presidency — Monroe refrained from openly asserting presidential influence, although he did work quietly behind the scenes.[47] The doctrine that bears Monroe's name was, as Ernest May has shown, the product of the highly political system within which his cabinet operated.[48] By accepting the independent roles of his department heads, Monroe further reinforced their independence and power. Under Jefferson, cabinet members in their contacts with Congress carried out the president's orders and wishes. Under Monroe, they used the resources of the executive to promote their own positions and future political prospects.

The shifting of political power from the president to Congress that had begun under Madison thus became far advanced under Monroe. Midway through Monroe's presidency, John Quincy Adams observed: "One of the most remarkable features of what I am witnessing every day is a perpetual struggle in both Houses of Congress to control the Executive — to make it dependent upon and subservient to them. They are continually attempting to encroach upon the powers and authorities of the President. As the old line of demarkation between parties has been broken down, personal has taken the place of principled opposition."[49] As president a few years later, Adams himself would feel the full brunt of that congressional power.

The decline of the nominating caucus ran counter to the growing power of Congress. That this should be the case was clear evidence of how weak the role of party had become. Without party purpose, the institutional weakness of the caucus was exposed. The caucus, in fact, had never gained complete acceptance; had never become fully institutionalized; and had never developed procedural stability. As James S. Chase has pointed out, nothing about the caucus was ever firmly established, not the time of meeting nor who was to call it.[50] And after 1812, its only formal machinery — a committee of correspondence and arrangement — was abandoned. In 1820, the caucus did not even make a nomination. An effort to revive the caucus, however, was made in 1824, but the much heralded overthrow of "King Caucus" was inevitable.

In the caucus of 1816, Crawford received only 11 fewer votes than Monroe, and Crawford and his friends believed that his acquiescence in the caucus decision gave him first claim to the nomination as Monroe's successor. As secretary of the treasury, Crawford had maintained his power base in Congress and, as the election of 1824 approached, most observers believed that he had the best prospect of winning caucus approval. The caucus system, which had been attacked every time it was employed, now became the main target of attack by the supporters of other candidates: Calhoun, Jackson, Clay, and Adams. These candidates were each placed in nomination by the legislatures or legislative caucuses in their home states, and each claimed this method of nomination was a better expression of popular sentiments than was the congressional caucus. After a group of 11 Crawford supporters in Congress issued a call for a caucus to meet in February 1824, another group of 24 members published a declaration announcing that 181 of the 261 members of both houses had given assurances that they deemed it "inexpedient, under existing circumstances", to meet in a nominating caucus and would not attend.[51] When the caucus met, only 66 members — slightly more than one-fourth of the two houses — attended. Ten states were not represented in the caucus, and two-thirds of those present came from four states.[52] Nevertheless, the caucus nominated Crawford for president. The caucus had acted, but its decision no longer carried any weight.

The breakup of the Republican party destroyed the only mechanism yet devised to provide for the nomination of presidential and vice-presidential candidates on a national level. The result was that in 1824 the electoral college operated for the only time in its history as the framers of the Constitution had anticipated, making only a preliminary screening of candidates and leaving the final decision to the House of Representatives. When the House decided the election in favor of John Quincy Adams, many refused to believe that this system was preferable to the discarded party system. The earlier conflict of the two great parties now appeared to be preferable to personal factions. Martin Van Buren would later reflect that the discreditable personal factionalism of the 1820s could have been avoided by the "steady adherence on the part of the Republican party to the caucus system."[53] Van Buren would be among those most active in restoring a party system to national politics.

The collapse of the caucus in 1824 was no sudden development, but was the final stage of the Republican party's disintegration, which had been under way since Madison's presidency. Only the threats of a Federalist revival had held the Republican party together under Madison. Once the War of 1812 was over and the Federalist party withdrew from national contention, the atrophy of the Republican party accelerated. Both on the national and state levels, a declining sense of party identity led to a collapse of party discipline, a slackening of party activity, and a deterioration of Republican party organization and machinery. The consequences of this were significant. In most states, where two parties no longer competed, there was a sharp decline in voter participation.[54] Not only had Federalists withdrawn from politics, but many Republicans had as well. In the presidential election of 1820, voter turnout reached a new low. In Baltimore, a city of over 62,000, only 568 persons voted. In Richmond, a city of 12,000, there were 17 votes cast, and only 4,321 persons voted in all of Virginia. Voters elsewhere displayed a similar lack of interest in voting in an election in which there was really only one candidate for president.[55]

Added to this was the changed environment in which politics operated. A much different nation existed in 1824 than existed in 1800: in size, distribution of the population, economic development, and national concerns. One dimension of the growth of the country could be seen in the increased membership of the House of Representatives from 106 in 1800 to 213 by 1824.

The nation was also distant from the critical party battle of 1800. In many of the new states, there had never been a party conflict between Federalists and Republicans. A changing constitutional and legal environment had also brought an expansion of the electorate by liberalizing suffrage requirements, a move away from the legislative choice of presidential electors, and an increase in statewide popular election of electors.

As long as the congressional caucus kept control of the presidential nominating process, the effects of these changes would not be fully felt. But once presidential contenders moved to seek support in constituencies outside Congress, as Calhoun, Jackson, Adams, and Clay did, they not only exposed the weakness of the caucus but laid the foundations for new parties and started a major transformation of U.S. politics.[56] The creation of a new party system restored under Jackson the presidential system to a vigor that would exceed its previous height under Jefferson. Had the congressional caucus been able to maintain control of the nominating process, it might not have preserved the Republican party, as Van Buren thought it might have, for the Republican party's decline was far wider than in Congress; but it almost certainly would have impeded the revival of presidential power. The demise of the caucus, therefore, had much meaning not only for the party process but for the larger U.S. political system.

Were the years between Jefferson and Jackson a period in which the U.S. constitutional structure drifted in the direction of a parliamentary system? The operation of the cabinet and the increasing dependence of the president and his ministers upon obtaining majorities in Congress to govern pointed in that direction, but two important trends ran counter to this. The first was the failure of the congressional caucus to maintain control over the presidential nominating process, leading to the involvement of broader segments of political leadership and the electorate in the process of selecting a president. The second was the continuing growth and differentiation of the committee system in Congress and the committees' expanding legislative oversight over executive departments. Nelson Polsby has argued that legislative committees "can be construed as fundamentally inimical to unified Cabinet government," because they give parliamentary parties the means to develop independent policy judgments, expertise, and oversight over the executive, and thereby threaten the cohesion of national political parties.[57] Congressional committees may thus be seen as affirming the independence of the legislature and at the same time acknowledging the independence of the executive, whose constitutional separateness made legislative vigilance essential.

The U.S. constitutional system under Monroe seems to have been heading less toward a parliamentary system than toward an ineffective republic in which the absence of a majority party and the growing factionalism of Congress made the process of policy agreement and legislating increasingly difficult. New York's Senator Rufus King described the Congress that met in 1821 at the beginning of Monroe's second term as "insipid and inefficient";[58] at the opening of this

Congress 12 ballots were needed to elect a Speaker. The most extensive study of the Congresses under Monroe argues that King's caustic description is applicable to Monroe's last four years in office. "The Congress directed its chief attention toward routine matters and theoretical questions on the nature of Congress and governmental institutions," writes George R. Nielsen. "Congressmen, instead of formulating policy, merely reacted to a variety of pressures. The legislators moved from issue to issue, from day to day, without discernible patterns."[59]

Rufus King claimed early in 1822 that President Monroe "tho' not buried is dead as respects direction, or control."[60] But in the end, members of Congress seemed less interested in establishing legislative supremacy than in determining who would next occupy the presidential office. What dominated Congress more than anything during Monroe's second term was maneuvering for the presidential election of 1824. The presidential system, it seems clear, had taken firm root. The effect of the attention of Congress to presidential politics in the 1820s was not to increase the role of Congress in the U.S. system of government, but, rather, to contribute to the reestablishment of political parties. This in turn led to the revival of presidential power.

The associations between presidential leadership and the strength and weaknesses of political parties during the period of the first party system were such as to suggest that, although vigorous political parties could not insure effective executive leadership, it would be difficult in the U.S. system for a president to be a strong leader without the support of a strong political party. Jefferson, the party leader, had provided the model of a president and Congress working successfully together. Madison and Monroe, adhering to the antiparty outlook that dominated their age, had revealed the difficulties faced by a president who did not have strong party support in Congress. John Quincy Adams, like his father before him, would refuse to accept the role of a party leader; Andrew Jackson would have no such reluctance. If Jackson did not restore the agrarian republic of Jeffersonian imagery, he did much to revive the party system of Jeffersonian realism.

NOTES

1. Charles Francis Adams, ed., *Memoirs of John Quincy Adams, Comprising Portions of His Diary from 1795 to 1848,* 12 vols. (Philadelphia: J. B. Lippincott, 1874-1877), Feb. 3, 1819, IV, 242.

2. Details on the caucus of 1804 can be found in Noble E. Cunningham, Jr., *The Jeffersonian Republicans in Power: Party Operations, 1801-1809* (Chapel Hill, N.C.: University of North Carolina Press, 1963), pp. 103-8.

3. At the opening of Congress in December 1801, there were 66 Republicans and 37 Federalists in the House, with two Republicans absent and one seat vacant. In the Senate, the party division was 18 Republicans and 14 Federalists. See Cunningham, *Jeffersonian Republicans in Power,* p. 71.

4. Further details and documentation can be found in Noble E. Cunningham, Jr., *The Process of Government under Jefferson* (Princeton, N.J.: Princeton University Press, 1978), pp. 244-45, 250-52, 323.

5. Ibid., pp. 282-87.

6. My reading of the evidence both in regard to boardinghouse blocs and the role of parties differs strongly from the conclusions in James Sterling Young, *The Washington Community 1800-1828* (New York: Columbia University Press, 1966). For further expansion of my arguments see Cunningham, *The Process of Government Under Jefferson,* pp. 272-78, 282-87.

7. Jefferson to Barnabas Bidwell, July 5, 1806, Thomas Jefferson Papers, Library of Congress.

8. Everett S. Brown, ed., *William Plumer's Memorandum of Proceedings in the United States Senate, 1803-1807* (New York: 1923), December 1, 1805, p. 337.

9. Jefferson to Wilson Cary Nicholas, April 13, 1806, in *The Writings of Thomas Jefferson,* ed. Paul L. Ford 10 vols. (New York: G. P. Putnam's Sons, 1892-1899), VIII, 435n.

10. Jefferson to Comte Destutt de Tracy, January 26, 1811, Ford, ed. *Writings of Jefferson,* IX, 307.

11. John Quincy Adams to his mother, April 23-May 16, 1817, Adams Papers, microfilm edition, reel 437, Columbia, MI: University of Missouri.

12. Archibald Henderson to Samuel Johnston, December 16, 1802, Hayes Collection, transcript, North Carolina Department of Archives and History.

13. Timothy Pickering to his wife, January 31, 1806, Timothy Pickering Papers, microfilm edition, reel 3.

14. Robert M. Johnstone, Jr., in *Jefferson and the Presidency: Leadership in the Young Republic* (Ithaca, N.Y.: Cornell University Press, 1978) applied Richard Neustadt's "bargaining model" to Jefferson's presidency and concluded that "Jefferson's presidency marked the pioneering effort in erecting a working model of presidential leadership characterized by persuasion and the cultivation of influence. Jefferson was the first president willing to implement the bargaining relationships that could enhance presidential influence" (p. 14).

15. Creed Taylor to unknown recipient, December 21, 1807, Creed Taylor Papers, University of Virginia.

16. Cabell to Nicholas, January 9, 1808, William H. Cabell Personal Papers, Miscellaneous, Library of Congress.

17. Samuel Taggart to Rev. John Taylor, January 27, 1808, in "Letters of Samuel Taggart, Representative in Congress, 1803-1814," ed. George H. Haynes, American Antiquarian Society, *Proceedings,* New Ser., 33 (1923), 303.

18. The caucus was reported in the *National Intelligencer* (Washington, D.C.), Jan. 25, 1808.

19. Thomas Leiper to Jefferson, received August 18, 1808, Jefferson Papers, Library of Congress.

20. Mitchill to his wife, November 23, 1807, Samuel L. Mitchill Papers, Museum of the City of New York.

21. Ralph Ketcham, *James Madison: A Biography* (New York, 1971), pp. 481-82.

22. Washington vetoed two bills; Adams and Jefferson vetoed none. *Presidential Vetoes: Record of Bills Vetoed and Action Taken thereon by the Senate and House of Representatives, First Congress through the Ninetieth Congress, 1789-1968,* compiled by the Senate Library (Washington, D.C.: Government Printing Office, 1969), pp. 1-3.

23. Madison to Jefferson, April 23, 1810, in *Letters and Other Writings of James Madison,* 4 vols. (Philadelphia: J. B. Lippincott, 1865), II, 472. See also Madison to Jefferson, February 7, 1812, ibid., 526.

24. Roger H. Brown, *The Republic in Peril: 1812* (New York: Columbia University Press, 1964), p. 45; Bradford Perkins, *Prologue to War: England and the United States, 1805-1812* (Berkeley, Calif., 1968), p. 410; Ronald L. Hatzenbuehler, "Party Unity and the Decision for War in the House of Representatives, 1812," *William and Mary Quarterly,* 3d. Ser., 29 (1972): 367-90.

25. Norman K. Risjord, "Election of 1812," in *History of American Presidential Elections,* ed. Arthur M. Schlesinger, Jr., and Fred L. Israel, 4 vols. (New York: Chelsea House-McGraw Hill, 1971), I, 250.

26. Harry Ammon, *James Monroe: The Quest for National Identity* (New York: McGraw-Hill, 1971), p. 354.

27. *Niles' Weekly Register* (Baltimore), 10 (1816): 59.

28. Ibid., 59-60.

29. Ammon, *Monroe,* p. 356.

30. Richard Hofstadter, *The Idea of a Party System: The Rise of Legitimate Opposition in the United States, 1780-1840* (Berkeley, Calif.: University of California Press, 1969), pp. 16, 22-24.

31. Monroe to Andrew Jackson, December 14, 1816, in *The Writings of James Monroe,* ed. Stanislaus M. Hamilton, 7 vols. (New York, 1898-1903), V, 345-46.

32. Ibid., 346.

33. Ibid., 342.

34. Samuel Dickens to his constituents, March 4, 1817, in *Circular Letters of Congressmen to Their Constituents, 1789-1829,* ed. Noble E. Cunningham, Jr., 3 vols. (Chapel Hill, N.C.: University of North Carolina Press, 1978), II, 1007.

35. Lewis Williams to his constituents, April 25, 1816, ibid., 980.

36. Norman K. Risjord, *The Old Republicans: Southern Conservatism in the Age of Jefferson* (New York: Columbia University Press, 1965), p. 180.

37. Mason to Rufus King, December 10, 1817, in *Louis McLane: Federalist and Jacksonian* by John A. Munroe (New Brunswick, N.J.: Rutgers University Press, 1973), p. 72.

38. Sanford W. Higginbotham, *The Keystone in the Democratic Arch: Pennsylvania Politics, 1800-1816* (Harrisburg, Pa.: Pennsylvania Historical and Museum Commission, 1952), p. 323; James A. Kehl, *Ill Feeling in the Era of Good Feeling: Western Pennsylvania Political Battles, 1815-1825* (Pittsburgh: University of Pittsburgh Press, 1956), pp. 90-91; Carl E. Prince, *New Jersey's Jeffersonian Republicans: The Genesis of an Early Party Machine, 1789-1817* (Chapel Hill, N.C.: University of North Carolina Press, 1967), pp. 182-202; Paul Goodman, *The Democratic-Republicans of Massachusetts: Politics in a Young Republic* (Cambridge, Mass.: Harvard University Press, 1964), pp. 202-4.

39. Joseph Story to Ezekiel Bacon, March 12, 1818, in *Life and Letters of Joseph Story*, ed. William W. Story, 2 vols. (Boston: Charles E. Little and James Brown, 1851), I, 311.

40. Bidwell to Jefferson, July 28, 1806, Jefferson Papers, Library of Congress.

41. Gallatin to Joseph H. Nicholson, January 19, 1802, in *The Writings of Albert Gallatin*, ed. Henry Adams, 3 vols. (Philadelphia: J. B. Lippincott, 1879), I, 74-75; Gallatin to Nicholson, April 1802, Joseph H. Nicholson Papers, Library of Congress.

42. Ammon, *Monroe*, p. 385.

43. Perry M. Goldman and James S. Young, eds., *The United States Congressional Directories, 1789-1840* (New York: Columbia University Press, 1973), pp. 81-82, 91-92, 417.

44. Leonard D. White compiled a list of 19 congressional investigations from 1815 to 1826. White, *The Jeffersonians: A Study in Administrative History, 1801-1829* (New York: Macmillan Co., 1951), pp. 99-100.

45. This interpretation differs from that in Young's *Washington Community* because Young rejected the role and importance of party under Jefferson and therefore was not concerned with the changing party conditions under Jefferson's successors.

46. Ammon, *Monroe*, pp. 384-85.

47. Ammon indicates that Monroe was in touch with Senator James Barbour of Virginia, an active figure in promoting compromise. Ibid., pp. 450-55.

48. Ernest R. May, *The Making of the Monroe Doctrine* (Cambridge, Mass.: Harvard University Press, 1975), pp. 256-57, 260.

49. Charles F. Adams, ed., *Memoirs of John Quincy Adams*, January 8, 1820, IV, 497.

50. James S. Chase, *Emergence of the Presidential Nominating Convention, 1789-1832* (Urbana, Ill., 1973), pp. 26-27.

51. *Anti-Caucus* [1824], broadside, New-York Historical Society.

52. *National Intelligencer* (Washington, D.C.), February 16, 1824.

53. Martin Van Buren, *Inquiry into the Origin and Course of Political Parties in the United States* (New York: Hurd and Houghton, 1867), p. 4; Hofstadter, *Idea of a Party System*, p. 229.

54. Richard P. McCormick, "Political Development and the Second Party System," in *The American Party Systems: Stages of Political Development,* ed. William Nisbet Chambers and Walter Dean Burnham (New York: Oxford University Press, 1967), pp. 95-96.

55. Charles S. Sydnor, "The One-Party Period in American History," *American Historical Review* 51 (1946): 442-43, 448.

56. As Richard P. McCormick has shown, the second American party system grew out of the contest for the presidency. Richard P. McCormick, *The Second American Party System* (Chapel Hill, N.C.: University of North Carolina Press, 1966), pp. 14-15.

57. Nelson W. Polsby, "The Institutionalization of the U.S. House of Representatives," *American Political Science Review* 62 (1968): 153.

58. Rufus King to Christopher Gore, February 3, 1822, quoted in George R. Nielson, "The Indispensable Institution: The Congressional Party during the Era of Good Feelings," (Ph.D. diss., University of Iowa, 1968), p. 130.

59. Ibid., pp. 130-31.

60. King to Gore, February 3, 1822, ibid., p. 130.

DISCUSSION OF THE CUNNINGHAM ESSAY

Austin Ranney

I am going to claim the chairman's privilege by asking the first question: Why did the caucus emerge in 1800? What needs did it meet? Why was it called forth?

Noble Cunningham

The very practical question of nominating candidates. Although Jefferson clearly was a consensus nominee — that is, the party clearly agreed upon Jefferson as the only candidate for president on the Republican side — there was no mechanism by which a vice-presidential candidate could be nominated. That question had been ignored in the election of 1796, and the result was the election of a president from one party and a vice-president from the other party. By 1800, parties had matured to the extent that they had become concerned with electing not one person but two, a president and a vice-president.

The Republican caucus met in 1800 specifically for the purpose of nominating Aaron Burr as vice-president. This was a political reward to Burr for carrying New York for the Republicans.

On the other hand, the Federalists used a caucus for the first and only time in 1800, and for them the problem was different. It grew out of the divisions within the Federalist party between Adams and Hamilton. The Federalist caucus resolved the problem by deciding to vote equally for Adams and Charles C. Pinckney. Hamilton's scheme to try to promote Pinckney above Adams came in the wake of the New York election when the Federalists now knew that they would not carry New York. Basically, immediate and practical problems led to both caucuses in 1800.

Richard McCormick

I think there is an important element missing from Noble's paper which bears upon the question that you raised, Austin, of why the caucus emerged in 1800. It also has an important bearing on the question that has been raised about attitudes toward parties. That missing ingredient is the Twelfth Amendment,

21

which was ratified in 1804. In the first place, the Twelfth Amendment constitutes a critically important recognition of party. The whole purpose of the Twelfth Amendment was to make possible partisanship in the contesting of the presidential elections, thereby reversing the position of the framers, who had so strenuously sought to devise a system that would be proof against parties.

With respect to why the caucus was so important in 1800, this was before the Twelfth Amendment. Therefore, it was absolutely essential, if the Republicans wished to secure both the presidency and the vice-presidency in 1800, that they have a management device that could insure that all Republican electors would agree on the same two individuals, and the most convenient one was the congressional caucus.

I think it is important in understanding the history of the caucus and its impermanence to see how its importance differed before and after the Twelfth Amendment. It was far more critical before than after the Twelfth Amendment, with its requirement of separate voting in the electoral college for president and vice-president. Thus, although the Twelfth Amendment provided a way of recognizing and even institutionalizing parties in the American constitutional system, in another sense it made the need for the caucus somewhat less urgent than had been the case in 1800.

James Banner

One of the central assumptions of the paper is that a party is essential to presidential leadership. Let's reverse the proposition. How strong would the Republican party have been without Jefferson as president? In some places, such as Pennsylvania or New York, there were certain states in which the Republican party no doubt would have proceeded without Jefferson's leadership. However, take New England and some of the regions of the South. What would have happened had Jefferson not been able to gain exposure in the press, had he not decided to push ahead with the Louisiana Purchase, and so on? Would there have been in fact a strong Republican party?

Noble Cunningham

I think it works both ways. Jefferson clearly contributed to a strong Republican party, and Madison contributed to the weakening of the party.

James Banner

In the absence of a Federalist president, it was impossible really for the Federalist party to get any kind of national momentum.

Noble Cunningham

That is true.

James Banner

I think it is important to bear this in mind. It is really a more dynamic circumstance than the initial pages of your paper suggest.

James Sundquist

My question is related to that one. I would like to hear historians expand on some aspects of this period that seem to have a particular bearing on the present day.

First, why did the Republican party disintegrate? You indicated at one point in your paper that it was largely due to Madison's lack of leadership on the Jeffersonian pattern, but you indicate elsewhere that the party was disintegrating all over the country anyway. I wonder what the balance might be between those forces, and whether what was going on then is analogous to what is going on in this country now.

Second, what brought about the revival of the party system after the disintegration? You do not get into that period in your paper but you touch on it a bit. If we could better understand what happened then, we might have a better feel as to whether our parties today can revive under analogous circumstances. Most political scientists seem to regard what is happening at the present time as a long-term trend leading to complete disintegration, rather than revival. What was it in 1828 or 1832 that turned the whole system around and brought about party revival?

Ronald Formisano

I think that there were probably some kind of parties present in 1800. Some scholars can accept the idea of parties existing in the early national periods, but not a system. In other words, parties, yes; a system, no. There were weak parties, striving to establish themselves. They were trying to make headway against the nonacceptance of parties and against everybody's assumption that parties were illegitimate and would someday fade away into one big party.

To make an even more basic point: When weak parties exist, then political events will have a much stronger impact. Administrations and even organizations designed to nominate candidates or mobilize the electorate were not so much independent variables as dependent variables. Historians have tended in recent years to reverse that process and to think that political organization is an independent variable. Indeed, it may be in certain periods of American history. But political organization is much more vulnerable to events. That is the way I would revise Professor Cunningham's statement. Why is partisanship intense at certain periods but not at others between 1800 and 1824? Because of events, one can see the Federalist party as a national organization just about going out of business by about 1804, becoming nonexistent at the national level as an organization. But about 1810 or 1811, the Federalists began to come back under the impact of political events. Then 1812 was the high water mark of partisanship and to some degree of national organization.

When do the parties go out of business? As soon as the foreign policy issues which have dominated the entire period and which have been the focal point of party polarization in Congress are disposed of — at that point party coherence began to collapse. One should not, however, call it a system, but "parties" begin to collapse after 1815.

I am advancing the general proposition that causality was not from parties and organizations to political events, but from political events and the political environment to parties.

Lee Benson

First, let me declare my interest. I have written a book that takes a position directly opposite to Noble's. My argument is essentially that the term "party" is hopelessly anachronistic before the 1830s. The reason for all the difficulty we are having in our discussion about "parties" in the early nineteenth century is that parties did not exist during that period. Partisan associations existed and factions existed. But to say that is basically different than to say that parties existed in the form that developed in the 1830s and 1840s. It is only when a mass electorate exists that actually is involved in politics that party organizations develop. That is quite distinct from the existence of factions, which had existed for hundreds of years.

I want to repeat my argument here because obviously it directly opposes Noble's proposition. I want to focus it by asking: In the early nineteenth century, did anybody really think that party was a good thing — party in terms of the organizational form that developed in the 1830s or 1840s — or did they regard parties as absolutely antithetical to the idea of the general commonwealth? When Jefferson was opposed to a Federalist faction, it was an *evil* faction which *represented* a narrow interest trying to subvert the entire commonwealth and the general interest. Until the idea exists that parties are legitimate, that there are necessary divisions within a complex society, that there are continuous, enduring group conflicts that can and should be organized in a sustained partisan political fashion, until then it seems to me hopelessly anachronistic to call the partisan associations anything but factions organized around temporary issues. I certainly agree with Ron Formisano's argument that is is only in respect to immediate particular foreign policy crises that something like a durable faction — and by that I mean one that lasted from two to three to four years — existed in the early nineteenth century. What did the congressional caucus do other than nominate candidates for the Republicans in perhaps two or three presidential elections? Did it actually function in any way between presidential elections?

Linda Kerber

It seems to me that one of the reasons we have problems dealing with the relationship of caucus to party is that we are not sure what that relationship is. In your paper, Noble, you are making caucus almost function as a metaphor for party. That is where we are having trouble. The caucus is not the party. It is an expression of partisanship inside Congress.

I think we should explore the distinction between the party as it functioned in Congress and the party as it functioned outside Congress. Was there a relationship of caucus to the great world outside? Was there a way in which people in the provinces hooked up to the caucus and found that it was meaningful to them? Or was it really a tactic or convenience which politicians found useful when they got to Washington?

Noble Cunningham

The caucus really did not do anything besides nominate candidates. It did appoint a committee, but that committee was concerned only with presidential elections. It was reconstructed only every four years. It did not have any ties to the electorate directly or to parties in states. Therefore, I would not over-emphasize the caucus in terms of the whole party system.

Certainly, the caucus was not the key. I do think it was extremely important because it represented the role of members of Congress in the party, but their role was broader than simply in the caucus. The caucus showed the importance of congressmen in the party, providing a kind of national organization. As an institution, the caucus itself has been overemphasized.

Linda Kerber

But not overemphasized as a device by which people who were not close to the center of the party could attempt to shape decisions. It seems to me that the major problem of that generation was to find devices by which outsiders, average or ordinary people, could affect the workings of government. Caucus was one, petitioning was one, and, eventually, mass political parties would be one. Is that a fair statement?

Noble Cunningham

To deal with the broader question, we have to get to the state level. There was a transition in the states during the period away from the role of caucus toward conventions, a process that directly involved larger numbers of voters. The national evolution from the congressional caucus to a national convention is a reflection of a transition that had taken place earlier in the states.

Judson James

I was struck by the point you were making here. Parties, I think, historically have developed from the national center. If you talk about the first-party system, you are talking about a national system. A first-party system is one at the national level. Not surprisingly, it is focused around foreign policy and a few domestic policy issues. When these issues wither, that system withers. However, something is going on. There is a diffusion of party outward. You start to build state and local party organizations, and when the national caucus goes out of business, the local party organizations survive.

We should not look solely at the national level. At the local level, Tammany Hall, even minus Burr, manages to continue. The courthouse gang in Charleston and other places in the country are still around. That begins to link into the revival of the second-party system. Over this period of time these party organizations at a local level are developing. They are around for Jackson and Van Buren to put together. The principal prize of politics is still the presidency. Therefore, those units need to relate and organize to it.

The party system disappears, but party organizations, without focus because of the lack of a national party system, continue to survive. In fact, they are growing through this period. They are becoming more significant. They are being fueled by the expansion of suffrage and other things.

I wonder whether this kind of transition — from a nationally developed system to a locally developed second system — is related to an interesting piece of data in your paper. You talk about the high level of turnover in the Congress going in at the beginning of the Monroe administration. One hundred twenty-six out of 185 are new members. I am curious as to how that relates to turnover in previous sessions. Is it markedly higher? Do you have explanations for the turnover? Might it not reflect the growth of the power of locally based party organizations to control and define what Congress is?

Richard McCormick

We are supposed to be concerning ourselves with this question of strong and weak parties. If we are going to try to talk about strong and weak parties in the period before 1824, then we have to make a distinction between the national level and the state level, as James Sundquist had already suggested.

Despite Noble's best efforts, I would have to conclude that parties in a national sense in that period were weak parties. Again, agreeing with the point Jim Banner made at least implicitly, a great deal of what seems to be the strength of the party in the Jeffersonian period is attributable to Jefferson.

On the other hand, one of the most neglected opportunities for analyzing strong and weak parties is to be found in that first-party system in terms of looking at individual states. I do not know whether Jim Banner would agree with me, but, with only a slight exaggeration perhaps, we might make the argument that Massachusetts never had stronger parties than it had between, say, 1804 and 1820. They were superbly organized parties with strong identification, high institutionalization, and close competition.

It might well be argued that we never came closer to a parliamentary kind of governmental system with an extremely strong party system than we did in Connecticut after 1810. It was probably the most advanced use of the legislative caucus, in the sense of parliamentary parties, that we have ever seen in America. It is possible, too, that a case might be made that you could scarcely find stronger parties than those that existed in Delaware from the late 1790s to the late 1820s. On the other hand, if one looks at Tennessee, Kentucky, Ohio, and a number of other states, there is hardly a vestige of party.

The point I am making is that the most profitable discussion of parties before 1824 probably has to focus on the experience in the states. Then, of course, the key question becomes one that is admittedly very difficult to address. Let us suppose we could agree that in Massachusetts between 1804 and 1824 we had very strong parties and in Tennessee we had none. What were the consequences in terms of policy outputs? How much difference did it make? What can we say about the consequences of parties in terms of meeting the demands that were circulating in the political system at the time? Unfortunately, there has not really been an approach to using that interesting laboratory provided by the variety of party situations to get at these questions of the effects of party.

Austin Ranney

You have just raised the key question of this whole conference: namely, What difference does it make? As a leading student of the period, what difference did the caucus's demise make?

Richard McCormick

Very little.

Arthur Link

It seems to me that the congressional caucus was potentially a viable instrumentality, given the primitive nature of parties during this period. This evolution toward creating an instrumentality for choosing a president certainly worked well in 1804. However, I think that the main question is why it failed. I do not think it failed because it was regarded at the time as undemocratic. This came later, after the caucus system had collapsed.

On account of peculiar circumstances, a number of weak presidents followed Jefferson. For all his intellect, I do not think anyone would ever claim that Madison was a strong president. Here we see already the beginning of the weakening and erosion of the caucus. Again, for various reasons which you have gone into, Noble, we get an even weaker president following Madison.

Obviously, the caucus system failed because it was unable to provide the strong national leadership which is absolutely essential to the successful working of parties, to say nothing of the successful administration of a government.

Gerald Pomper

There is a question prior to whether the parties then were strong and weak. Lee Benson has questioned whether there were parties at all. The problem of definition is thus critical here. If you think of parties as a special kind of organization, then you can use definitional criteria of what organizations are, and then determine whether or not parties meet these criteria.

Although the parties were weak in many respects, it seems to me they had the essential characteristics of organizations. You just mentioned four or five. One is recognized leadership. It seems clear that the parties in the early 1800s had that. Another is continuity and a means of selecting continuing leadership. The caucus provided that, at least for a time. Behavioral unity is another test of an organization. We see that to some extent both in Congress and in the electoral college in the caucus period. Among voters we see a lot. Some defined hierarchy, some differentiation of functions, is another criterion. Most importantly, party organization is an extension of centralized leadership organs out into what, at the time, is a mass electorate. That is the purpose of the party.

If you look at what defines an organization, parties at this time — especially the Republican party — had those characteristics. Therefore, the definitional question ought to be resolved and we should say; "Yes, they were organizations. They did not do their jobs very well. They did not continue as long as they might, but they surely were organizations." Therefore, there was a party system then, even if it was not the fully matured party system that developed later on.

Ronald Formisano

I think it ought to be said in fairness to Noble Cunningham that throughout American history there have been very incomplete party systems. If one looks just at the state level, for example, as Dick McCormick was suggesting, and if one uses the criterion of competitiveness, one can find many noncompetitive states throughout the entirety of American history. I would agree that in Massachusetts there were relatively well-developed parties.'If one looks at the South, one finds nothing. There have been studies of roll call voting in the South Atlantic legislatures which show that parties did not function in the South Atlantic legislatures. I think Noble Cunningham's recent edition of the circular letters of Congressmen to their constituents shows that same thing about the South and West. In Delaware and Maryland, indeed, you do find very well-developed parties, and in New Jersey, too. I would very strongly disagree about Connecticut. In Connecticut, local issues — especially the religious issue — caused very high turnout at a time when the parties were dying elsewhere. So Connecticut moved to an entirely different beat. Contrary to the usual picture of New York and Pennsylvania being big states, heterogeneous, complex, and producing parties, New York and Pennsylvania really do not hold a candle to New Jersey, Maryland, Delaware, or Massachusetts. New Hampshire and Vermont are also not very well developed.

Several recent studies at the state level show that local origins are extremely important in the genesis of state parties. Those studies also take into account national issues, and show that when those national issues departed, the organizations likewise collapsed. I would stress, as Gerald Pomper has stressed in his work criticizing *The American Voter,* that as the political context or political environment was ignored in the classic voting studies of the 1950s, so has the political context and the political environment been ignored in the early national period.

Donald Robinson

I would like to make a remark or two relating the conduct of politics between 1800 and 1824 to the Federal convention that framed the Constitution. We have here an account of the development of the recruitment process, and we know something about, and the performance of, those presidents — Jefferson, Madison, and Monroe — once in office. I would like to relate that to the intention of the framers.

The truth is that the framers gave very little thought to the question of the recruitment of presidents. There is an astonishing glibness and superficiality in the framers' thought concerning the election of presidents. That is what is impressive in reading through Madison's notes and the other sources we have on this question. It is almost impossible to make sense of the intentions of the framers. The truth is there was no intelligent or developed intention at all about how presidents should be chosen.

However, the initial effect of their design, as Professor Cunningham makes clear, was to encourage the ties that they deplored and that they hoped to prevent from developing; namely, ties between Congress and the presidency. If they had a fundamental intent regarding the recruitment of the presidency, it was to prevent corruption that they thought would inevitably arise if there were ties, relationships, and dependencies developed between the president and a faction or a party in Congress. They feared presidential weakness, and they feared corruption. They thought both would develop if the presidency were made dependent upon Congress.

The method that developed — the caucus system — precisely frustrated this intention. (As I have argued, it was not a very well-developed intention.) This situation was not remedied until constituency parties — popular parties — developed through the extraconstitutional conventions as a mechanism for remedying the defect in the framers' design. The effect of the development of these conventions and the second party system was, ironically, to restore the framers' most fundamental intent; namely, that the executive and the legislative be separated and "march to a different drummer."

I would make one other comment related to this. Jim Banner has stressed the dialectical relationship — the dynamic relationship — between a strong party and a strong presidency, suggesting that causalities run both ways. Another way of saying that is to say that you will have neither a strong party nor a strong presidency without strong links between the president and a popular constituency party.

The exception to that is Thomas Jefferson, but I would suggest that he is an exception that proves the rule. I think no one here is arguing that strongly developed constituency parties existed under Jefferson. What you had was a man who had a relationship to the nation based upon his involvement in the Revolution and his reputation. Therefore, there was a powerful relationship between Jefferson and the nation which existed even though strongly articulated constituency parties did not exist.

Madison and Monroe well illustrate the difficulties of a presidency which does not have strong ties to a constituency party, which is dependent upon nomination from a congressional caucus, and which gets tangled up in the corruption and weakness which the framers anticipated would attend a presidency emerging from the Congress.

The period between 1800 and 1824 suggests that without strong linkages between a president and a popular party, there cannot be strong parties; there cannot be a strong presidency; and, following the Hamiltonian argument, we cannot have energetic government.

Robert McClory

I did not sense that there was really any inherent strength in the congressional caucus. Their strength appears to be associated with the president. In other words, when Jefferson was president and he invited members of Congress to the White House three nights a week to have dinner, the party was strong. It gave him strong support in his reelection campaign. However, later, when Monroe denounced the caucus, it did not have any strength of its own from which to fight back, but tended to disappear.

Frequently we hear that the Constitution does not provide for political parties so we had to invent them. I think the congressional caucus was the early invention and the development of the political parties was the later invention to fill a vacuum so that this system of government, which we have lived under now for approaching 200 years, has been able to demonstrate a great vitality.

I was struck by the fact that following Jefferson's departure the voter participation was dismally small, perhaps the lowest in our entire history, as you brought out in examples of Richmond, Virginia, and Baltimore, Maryland. Perhaps we find some correlation with today. With the reduced influence of the political parties, as you brought out, Austin, there is likewise a corresponding reduction in voter participation. In other words, as the strong party organization loses its strength, the force that gets out the vote seems to disappear and fewer persons participate in the election. While we may applaud the increase in independent voters, it likewise seems to have been accompanied by apathy or indifference to participation in the political system.

Kay Lawson

I have been very happy to see the emphasis upon constituency links and the question of whether we can properly talk about strong parties before we can identify that there are such constituency links. I have not been surprised, but I have been a little distressed, to see the emphasis upon the idea that these links must be with the presidency. I would like us to return, just briefly, to the question of Congress and the role that Congress as an institution, not simply the congressional caucus, played in the development of strong parties.

I would argue that during this period, parties were beginning to form within the national institutions and within the states, but that there was no organized party system. I am not convinced by those who suggest that a few years later we did have a strong party system. My position is that, given the weakness of constituency links, we have yet to have strong parties or a strong party system.

I wonder if the failure of Congress as an institution which could facilitate the growth of strong parties did not begin in this era. I thought Noble

Cunningham's comments on the decline of the caucus were very interesting. I was not sure whether he was saying "because of" or "simultaneously with" the decline of the caucus that two things were happening: First, the nomination of the president was moving away from the caucus and going outside into the more general populace with the convention system; secondly, within Congress strong committees began to develop. He moved away from that rather quickly, but he did say that Congress was not developing as a strong institution controlling policy questions.

I think all of these questions are linked. Some people have said − and I agree − that strong parties mean aggregating interests. We cannot look to a president as the single national institution to aggregate interests. He is only one person. However, Congress is also an institution supposedly designed to aggregate interests. How can we have strong parties without a strong Congress? What happened in this period that related to that question of links between parties and Congress? Why did the caucuses − and Congress − decline, rather than prosper?

Arthur Link

May I speak to that? If American history demonstrates anything, it demonstrates that Congress, for all its virtues in a balanced system of government, has never been capable of giving national leadership. On rare occasions there may be exceptions. Obviously, a Congressman's primary responsibility is to his district, a Senator's to his state. Theoretically and idealistically, all Congressmen and Senators are supposed to represent the national interest, but in practice it has never been that way, and I do not think it ever will be that way.

We have not had many successful administrations − maybe four, five, or six. These successful administrations have occurred only when there has been a dynamic, strong president standing, as it were, above particular interests, and reconciling, uniting, harmonizing, and getting the party to pull together behind a constructive program to meet particular needs. This happened under Jefferson. I would say that it did not happen again until Wilson.

If this paper demonstrates anything, it demonstrates the incapacity of Congress − whether through caucus, committee, or what have you − truly to govern the country without that strong, unifying, constructive, innovative moving force which inheres in the presidency. This is true because the presidency is, as Wilson said, the one institution in which inheres the basic sovereignty of the whole people. Is that not true?

Kay Lawson

It is true, but what does it mean for parties?

Arthur Link

It means a great deal for parties. It means that when you have a strong presidency, you have a strong party. For example, in the case of Wilson, the Democrats in Congress had been divided into factions since 1893. Then there came a man who somehow, miraculously, was able to pull all these disparate groups together into a tightly knit team. (It was not miraculous; it was all deliberate and planned. Wilson knew exactly what he was doing.) In other words, our system has worked only when we have had a president such as Wilson, Jefferson, and Franklin Roosevelt who was a master of the parliamentary process.

Richard Abrams

I would like to get back to these kinds of issues: What are the consequences in terms of social policy and organization of a strong or weak party system? In other words, what can we expect when a party organization or system is weak and what can we expect when they are strong? What can history tell us about these things?

Everett Ladd

A while ago, Richard McCormick noted that we had both strong and weak parties in the period about which we are talking. There was a very strong party arrangement in Massachusetts, whereas it was weak or even nonexistent in Tennessee. The comparisons are interesting. When pushed, Professor McCormick said that he did not think it made much difference whether we were operating under a strong party in Massachusetts or a weak party in Tennessee.

I would like to see if he and others could pursue this a bit further. Does a strong or weak party make any difference, and by what standards? For example, is one of the standards: How effective is popular control? What would the list of standards be? Would they be the same standards that we would want to employ today in evaluating whether or not it makes a difference to have strong or weak parties? It might not make any difference in terms of those standards in one period, but it might make a great deal of difference in terms of those standards in another period, because the context is so very important. What needs to be done presumably varies greatly from one context to another.

Richard McCormick

If we are concerned about the extent of participation in a nonparty context, it is quite remarkable that in Tennessee, which really had nothing approaching organized parties before 1835, voter participation was remarkably high. Similarly, in Alabama in the 1820s, where there were no parties, participation was strangely high. I say "strangely" because it is difficult to explain readily why this was the case. From what I have been able to learn about what policy outputs were, in Alabama or Tennessee they seemed to have met reasonable expectations. Of course, if we try to link that observation with the whole series of studies that have flowed out of Richard Dawson, James Robinson, Thomas Dye, and others trying to identify the effects of political variables on policy outputs, we are perhaps less astonished at the performance of these nonparty politics than we might have been twenty years ago.

William Keefe

Professor Cunningham began his remarks by saying that sooner or later we would have to address ourselves to the tasks of identifying what constitutes a strong party system or a weak party system. It occurs to me that very close to the top of the list of indicators of a strong party system would be significant differences in policy attitudes in Congress — that is to say, the kind of evidence that one would find in roll call votes on various kinds of policy questions. I want to ask whether there is any evidence to suggest the character of interparty conflict in the Jeffersonian period.

If you say there were some meaningful differences, and that they involved more than foreign policy questions, then there is support in your paper for the proposition that strong electoral parties are really not required to have strong party performances in Congress. Is there evidence of policy conflict in the Jefferson period as measured by congressional voting?

Noble Cunningham

We need more roll call analysis. There has been little roll call analysis of the Jeffersonian period. It may not interest scholars because of the imbalance of seats between the Federalists and the Jeffersonians. We do not have the information to answer your question fully.

William Keefe

The most interesting idea I found in your paper is that we ought to emphasize the separateness of electoral parties and congressional parties. It may be that the separateness of these two entities creates a condition under which meaningful party differences can develop in Congress on various kinds of policy questions, even though in the electorate the parties are in the process of dying.

My summary point is this: Party began in Congress. In my view, Congress is the last bastion. Indeed, a good deal of party decay can occur in the electorate and we can still have meaningful, reasonably responsible party performance in Congress. It seems to me that even though the 1960s and 1970s were particularly hard on the electoral parties, party performance in Congress in fact changed very little. In terms of roll call votes, there was not much difference in party performance in the mid-70s as compared with the mid-1960s. Similarly, in the early 1800s, there were significant party differences in Congress even though there were no important linkages between the congressional caucus and the constituencies.

Ronald Formisano

The roll call analysis that we do have suggests that the period from 1809 to 1815 was about the only time that there were policy differences. They were on a couple of sets of issues. In 1812, what many historians have called the zenith of parties existed in Congress — the height of partisan conscientiousness. In fact, the vote on the war was much motivated by a desire to preserve the Republican party, and that is about as far as it went in this early period in terms of deliberate, self-conscious, party consciousness.

However, look at the presidential election that year. A small, self-selected group of Federalists met secretly and decided to nominate no one, so that the way would be open for some local Federalist cadres to support DeWitt Clinton, a maverick Republican, in New York State. If one looks at voting returns in the states in 1812, one finds office-specific electoral coalitions. There was almost no relationship between who was voting for Congress, president, and so on.

Patricia Bonomi

Enlightening as the comments have been, they have demonstrated the difficulty of connecting parties of the early national years to those of a later time. This occurs in part because we are dealing with a difference in kind. At least three elements, all of which have been mentioned in some manner this morning, differentiated the parties, or factions, of this early period from later ones.

The first was, of course, limited suffrage. Property qualifications for voters, inadequate systems of communication and travel, and habits of political apathy all restricted suffrage, inhibiting the growth of grass roots parties and organized competition at the local level. Another difference relates to the type of person expected to hold public office. The early nineteenth century was still an age of deference, though attitudes were changing as the political base gradually broadened with the extension of suffrage. It was not until the 1830s and 1840s, however, that such changes were sufficiently apparent to transform public consciousness.

The third and most important element was the inability of a generation of Revolutionaries turned Founding Fathers to conceive of a loyal opposition, to recognize that the "outs" could serve as a rein on the "ins," and that this might be one more device for balancing and checking power. It is the eventual acceptance of the legitimacy of a loyal opposition that finally draws parties into the constitutional system.

Party, as defined by Professor Cunningham, involves a series of power relationships within Congress and their interactions with the executive branch. As our discussion moves on to later periods of American history, the definition of party will expand as these original centers of power form links with grass roots political organizations and interest groups at the state and local levels.

2

TWO TRADITIONS OF PROGRESSIVE REFORM, POLITICAL PARTIES, AND AMERICAN DEMOCRACY

David P. Thelen

During the period from 1880 to 1920, local, state, and national governments enacted more measures to change the formal political activities of voters, politicians, legislators, political parties, and public administrators than in any comparable era in the nation's history. These changes eroded the power and autonomy of nineteenth century political leaders and have thus passed into political history, lumped together, as the "progressive reforms." There are two problems with this. By treating all of these changes as parts of a single, monolithic progressive movement, the prevailing emphases fail to recognize that the changes pointed in two very different directions: one toward democracy and another toward bureaucracy. By treating the reforms as part of a static reform challenge that did not alter emphases and programs, the prevailing emphases overlook important modifications that reformers made in their programs. The two traditions of political reform in this period remain the two basic challenges to politics today, and by treating them as changing and evolving traditions we can try to build from them in the future.

All political reformers of this period developed their programs in response to a unique fact about the American political environment. In 1880, all classes of males, poor as well as rich, held the right to vote *before* the rapid spread of large-scale industrial capitalism and its major agent, the large corporation.

Note: I would like to thank Gerald Pomper, Judson James, and Austin Ranney for directing me to literature critical of initiatives, Otis Graham for spirited criticism, and, especially, Robert H. Wiebe for suggesting ways of making the argument more effective.

By contrast, new industrial workers in other parts of the world encountered industrialization before they had representative government. Karl Marx and Frederick Engels observed, for example, that the world's first self-conscious proletariat, the British Chartists, formed around the demand for the ballot.[1] But in the United States, the ballot preceded the factory, mill, and mine. Universal manhood suffrage had led to the systematic, grassroots development of political parties by 1880, and it was never far from the minds of reformers as they sought to reshape the political system to meet the new challenges created by maturing industrial capitalism.

The two different traditions of political reform in this period resulted from two very different ways of evaluating the effect of large-scale industrial capitalism on a political process in which rich and poor alike held the vote. Although some groups worked solely to advance such single causes as civil service reform, direct legislations, and woman suffrage and some reforms incorporated elements of both reform traditions, the issues that reformers promoted finally resolved into two conflicting approaches. The pattern of the two traditions was that of two overlapping circles. Within each circle were smaller dots that represented particular reform programs, and the edges of the two circles overlapped. But they had separate and distinct cores. And the cores that defined programs as part of one circle or the other emerged around the issues of corporate and voter influence.

The first reform tradition emphasized the desirability of infusing more values, methods, and personnel from the business community into traditional political practices. Its reforms promoted such basic corporate values as efficiency, production, planning, centralization, nonpartisanship, hierarchy, administration, expertise, and stability against prevailing practices that exalted partisanship, majority rule, decentralized power, legislation, and voter participation — particularly participation by poorer voters.

Equally hostile toward prevailing political habits, the second reform tradition sought to fulfill the nation's democratic heritage by depriving corporations of political influence. These reforms were indifferent to partisanship as such and exalted, instead, the voter and majority rule. They tended to encourage decentralization and equality over centralization and hierarchy, consumption over production, and legislator over administration.

Both traditions built their programs from a variety of groups that challenged partisan political activities in the late nineteenth century. From their scattered roots in the late nineteenth century, both groups reached their fullest development — and the enactment of their basic programs — in the early twentieth century. Neither reform tradition defied all features of prevailing politics. This essay will explore the diverse sources of each tradition and trace its evolving contribution to the transformation of U.S. politics in this period.

THE CORPORATE AND BUREAUCRATIC TRADITION

The earliest and most obvious shapers of the bureaucratic tradition were businessmen and corporations that simply wanted public policy and political practice to meet their needs. The political system offered them many advantages and opportunities, as Moisei Ostrogorski observed, to mold policy making to their basic drive for profit.[2] They had a century-old tradition reaching back at least to the Constitution, as Charles A. Beard and J. Allen Smith argued, of promoting changes in governmental structures to limit democratic pressures on politics embodied in the Declaration of Independence.[3] The structural changes advocated by businessmen shared with prevailing political practices the common values of hierarchy and capitalism. From this point of view, political competition was like economic competition. Politicians were merchants who owned a certain number of votes as capital to trade for public offices that society treated as things that had to be paid for.[4] Like the businessman who needed constantly expanding capital to compete effectively, the political leader required an ever-increasing amount of money to defeat competitors in the frequent and expensive elections the political leader tried to manage. Politicians paid for these elections by rewarding campaign workers with public offices and then taking part of each officeholder's salary. The competition for buying and selling votes took place within a hierarchical structure, from precinct leader to local and state "boss," in which the fittest clawed to the top. The successful politician shared basic values with the successful businessman.

The prevailing political system of 1880 likewise offered golden opportunities to the new corporations. As the only agencies to unite U.S. citizens across social and geographic barriers, commanding loyalty and discipline among their ranks, political parties were tailor made for the new corporations and their demands for franchises, tax incentives, tariffs, and other public policies. Instead of having to persuade millions of isolated and diverse voters or dozens of equally diverse legislators, the increasingly far-flung corporations had only to reach a few prominent political leaders to reap rewards.[5]

Whatever values and mutually profitable arrangements corporate leaders might share with political leaders, however, many businessmen recognized that the differences between their drive for profits and the politicians' drive for office created inherent problems. Corporate leaders feared, above all, that politicians might attack corporate practices in their quests for votes. The bitter anti-railroad movements of the 1870s that produced the Granger laws and other measures to tax and regulate the railroads, first of the large corporations, profoundly frightened the new corporate officials as a harbinger of future problems in a political system based on universal manhood suffrage.[6] Corporate officials realized that to receive favorable consideration from politicians, especially at times and places where corporate practices were unpopular, they would need to develop methods that would make political leaders dependent on corporations for the basic tools of the political trade, as they had made workers dependent on corporations for their tools. The basic solution was to modify the patronage system in ways that would shift the dependency of politicians from patronage workers to corporations for the costs of financing elections. The Pendleton Act of 1883, which inaugurated the process of converting federal public jobs from patronage rewards to civil service appointments, served corporate needs perfectly when it prohibited politicians from assessing public employees for costs of elections.[7] As the civil service reform movement spread to cities and states over the next two decades, businessmen frequently offered not only to pay for elections but also to hire faithful party workers for their street carlines, railroads, and other corporations. Corporations came to replace government as the patronage trough, particularly for municipal jobs, thereby cementing bonds between corporations and political leaders. Corporations incorporated political leaders into managerial positions for the sole purpose of exploiting their political influence for corporate profits; and, finally, many businessmen began to participate actively in party councils in the hope of gaining immunity for their corporations.[8] They made close alliances with political bosses like Republican Henry C. Payne in Milwaukee, Democrat Edward Butler in St. Louis, and Union Labor Abe Ruef in San Francisco.[9]

But the basic barrier to a full amalgamation of corporations and politicians was that politicians owed their first obligations to their parties, businessmen to their corporations. As a result, their objectives were always potentially antagonistic. The new corporate leaders dared not make too close an alliance with a single party, because they feared that party might lose the next election. Corporations were inherently nonpartisan or bipartisan. "In a Republican district I was a Republican; in a Democratic district I was a Democrat; in a doubtful district I was doubtful; but always I was Erie," confessed Erie railroad leader Jay Gould.[10] The Milwaukee streetcar and lighting monopoly made Republican boss Henry C. Payne its chief executive officer and gave its second spot to Democratic boss Edward C. Wall.[11] Even as they made alliances with leaders of particular parties, corporate managers yearned for more permanent methods of public administration that would immunize them from the two things they could not control: hostile voters, and politicians whose first allegiances were to their parties.

The particular forms of the structural changes that weakened the power of voters and partisanship came not so much from corporations as from a series of reform movements that evolved from the 1800s to the 1900s. Although businessmen played disproportionately large roles in these movements, particularly in their earlier years, the reformers were more concerned with limiting the political influence of partisanship and poor voters than they were with advancing corporate profits. They were eager to create a society governed by merit, and they frequently considered independent professionals to be at least as worthy as businessmen. Many would have preferred to exalt the ideal of the aristocrat over that of the businessman in the 1880s, but this was politically impossible with universal manhood suffrage, and politically undesirable when businessmen were their most likely allies.

To create a political system based on merit, these reformers constantly contrasted the successful businessman with the successful politician. Measuring political performance against the yardstick of the businessmen, these reformers concluded that partisanship was the basic problem in politics. The political system encouraged only the value of party loyalty, whereas the competitive world of business bred for talent, integrity, intelligence, and experience. In contrast to businessmen who always had to reduce labor costs to remain competitive, politicians seemed ever eager to create unnecessary jobs — at great expense to taxpayers — to have places for the party's election workers. Since party loyalty was the only prerequisite for public employment, patronage appointees were generally incompetent and frequently corrupt, the reformers reasoned.[12]

The first program for many of these reformers was civil service reform because it would base public employment on the business ideal of competition, instead of on the political ideal of loyalty. Civil service reform would reorganize politics along corporate lines by making competence and expertness the basis for employment by weakening the power of politicians and by removing the incentive to create unnecessary jobs to reward the party faithful, thereby lowering the tax burden of businessmen. Corporations would replace officeholders as the politicians' main financial supporters. Beginning in 1883 with the United States Civil Service Commission and that same year with a similar New York State Commission, the civil service reform movement grew steadily over the next 25 years, depriving politicians of the basic Jacksonian tool of their trade.

Early reformers in the bureaucratic tradition pushed other structural changes to erode partisanship. Beginning on a large scale in the 1880s, they insisted that partisanship was particularly irrelevant to local issues and that the introduction of national party labels and issues to local elections provided, in the words of the Ashland, Wisconsin, Civic Federation "the screen behind which the systematic plundering of the city is accomplished."[13] The early reformers crusaded to have municipal elections conducted on a nonpartisan basis at different times of year from state and national elections in the hope of persuading voters that city governments were essentially business corporations whose performance should be evaluated by business, not partisan, values. By 1913, California, for example, required that all local, county, school, and judicial offices be elected on a nonpartisan basis.[14] Although Minnesota even elected its state legislature by nonpartisan ballot in the 1900s, the movement for nonpartisan elections was basically confined to the local level. The reason for this was that city governments were, in fact, far more administrative and therefore were closer to the corporate ideal than were state and national governments. As a result, municipal politics more often revolved around competition between the party in power and independent antimachine movements than between the two major parties.[15]

Striving to enshrine the values of the large corporations, these reformers believed that the structures of government were too democratic and uncoordinated, that they were not hierarchical enough in fixing executive responsibility for administration. They campaigned simultaneously to strengthen the executive branches of government at the expense of more democratic legislatures, to establish hierarchical chains of command within executive branches, and to change the method for choosing administrators from popular election to administrative appointment. The movement for a shorter ballot, for example, was a movement to make public administrators responsible to other administrators instead of to voters. The myriad charter reforms for large cities, such as those for Boston, Philadelphia, and Los Angeles in the mid-1880s, strengthened the mayor's control over administration at the expense of city councils.[16]

By the early twentieth century, municipal reformers in this tradition brought together many of the isolated late nineteenth century reform causes into single new proposals that combined and extended their separate campaigns while preserving the older reformers' faith that corporate organization was more efficient, therefore more desirable, than that of parties. Even the strong mayors sought by late nineteenth century reformers were too democratic because they were elected, frequently on partisan tickets, so voters and parties still wielded too much power. Beginning with commission government in Galveston, Texas, in 1901, and city manager government in Staunton, Virginia, in 1908, these new government structures merged many important themes in the bureaucratic reform tradition. They transferred power from the local wards to citywide offices, from voters to administrators, from patronage to merit, from partisan politicians to nonpartisan managers, from city council debate among equal aldermen to hierarchical chains of administrative command — in short, from democracy to efficiency. Even in cities that did not fully transfer all supervisory power to appointed administrators, reformers successfully created nonpartisan commissions to make and enforce policies in specialized areas such as police, fire, welfare, transportation, taxation, recreation, sanitation, and housing.[17] These new city charters of the early twentieth century thus represented the fullest expression of the bureaucratic tradition of municipal reform as they enacted the values of efficiency, nonpartisanship, planning, centralization, hierarchy, administration, and expertise.

Bureaucratic reformers transformed the political and administrative forms of U.S. cities. In 1880, cities elected their officials on partisan ballots to represent local wards in powerful city councils. By 1922, 489 cities had converted to the commission form and 240 to the city manager form of government. Although commission governments eroded partisanship and neighborhood political power, they were still accountable directly to voters, and administration remained divided among the three to seven elected commissioners. For this reason, many bureaucratic reformers turned their energies toward the city manager system that established hierarchical administration removed at least one step from voter control while also weakening the power of political parties and neighborhoods. Reflecting the bureaucratic reformers' increasing enthusiasm for manager, instead of commission, governments, the commission form attracted 245 cities between 1911 and 1913 and the manager form only 11 over the same three years, but in the three years between 1920 and 1922, 108 cities adopted the manager form and only 14 the commission form. The first *Municipal Year Book,* published in 1934, traced the full dimensions of the bureaucrats' accomplishments during the Progressive Era. By 1933, only 49 percent of the 190 cities with over 50,000 people retained the mayor-council form; 28 percent were governed by commissions and 23 percent by managers. Fifty-nine percent of cities over 50,000 elected their officials on nonpartisan ballots and the same percentage elected a majority of their representatives on a citywide basis. Only one-quarter of all cities in 1933 elected all of their councilmen or commissioners from the wards.[18]

The creation of strong, independent administrators free from both partisan and voter control were facets of a struggle over who would have the knowledge and information necessary to govern. Once again, the reformers took their basic ideas from developments in corporate administration. The basic principle of scientific corporate management that the reformers applied to public administration was that of efficient production. The key to efficient production was to expropriate the traditional knowledge of workers and, through superior capital resources, reorganize that knowledge and impose it from above through administrative chains of command. Frederick W. Taylor explained that "the [corporate] managers assume . . . the burden of gathering together all of the traditional knowledge which in the past has been possessed by the workmen and then of classifying, tabulating, and reducing this knowledge to rules, laws, and formulae" to govern the plant from above.[19]

The bureaucratic reformers used the new governmental machinery to transfer the experiences, feelings, and power of voters, city employees, amateur volunteers, and politicians to nonpartisan administrative experts who would gather information and reduce it to rules and regulations. The first stage in the evolution of the independent expert lay in the creation of agencies of applied research that would evaluate governmental performance against the corporate model of efficient production. The most widely copied agency of this type was the New York Bureau of Municipal Research, formally established in 1907, according to its chief architect William H. Allen, to "apply the disinterestedness of research, and the techniques of business management, to public affairs and civic problems."[20] By collecting information and developing programs in areas like housing, health, and, particularly, budgeting and taxation, this New York bureau and its imitators in Philadelphia, Cincinnati, Chicago, Milwaukee, and other cities provided not only the link between corporations and reformers but also "contributed considerably to the transformation of the moral precept of honest government into the scientific notion of efficient business management."[21] The same processes applied at the state level to agencies like the

Wisconsin Legislative Reference Library and at the federal level to agencies like the Census Bureau.[22]

The capstone of the process by which these reformers transformed the system of public administration from partisanship and democracy to their cherished ideals of bureaucracy and efficiency was the independent regulatory commission. Staffed at least in theory by nonpartisan experts, these regulatory commissions formed the uniquely U.S. solution to the problem of public control over large-scale enterprise. Few historians, not even Gabriel Kolko, would deny that the political situation that created these commissions was one of massive popular protests against new corporate practices.[23] Few political scientists would deny that the commissions in practice have not basically represented the unorganized majority. Instead, as Marver Bernstein argued in his classic study, commissions have been captured by the very industries they were designed to regulate.[24]

The apparent contradiction between democratic origins and corporate practice melts when the regulatory commissions are viewed not as objectives of particular corporations but as a further application of the bureaucratic model at the time when the ever dangerous fact of universal manhood suffrage was converted into unprecedented popular hostility to corporate practices. It was precisely the partisan and democratic political setting shaped by muckraking journalists, legislative investigations of corporate practices, vote hungry politicians, and general anger of consumers that most deeply troubled champions of regulation when they promoted the new commissions. "Is it any wonder," asked Charles McCarthy, chief ideologue of the Wisconsin Idea regulators, "that the business man is afraid of a legislative session when every bolt or screw in his machinery may be regulated by impractical laws or matters or actuarial skill be determined in a few moments in a legislative committee, or the price of gas or some other thing equally scientific, regulated in an equally crude manner?"[25] Proof of the superiority of independent regulation was documented by the lower rate of business failures was lower in Wisconsin than in less regulated states. Since Wisconsin regulations "are made to fit into the harmony of industrial conditions," contended McCarthy, "greater advances can be made than by following the wild shouts of reformers who would destroy without constructing."[26]

Behind the regulators' championship of growth, applied science, and administration against the demagogic, partisan, and radical legislators was a fundamental clash over the meaning of expertise. The clash differed from the anger that workers felt when corporate officials used their knowledge against them. In the clash over regulatory commissions, many people practically begged the regulators to listen to their complaints and formulate administrative rules based on that information. The battle over the meaning of expertise was actually a battle over whether government should base policies on needs of producers or needs of consumers. Relying on a corporate model of administration, regulators emphasized efficient production as the highest good because it created the greatest growth; they were experts in the narrow details of the prevailing productive processes. Regulators burned with a passion to halt waste, whether it was unnecessary patronage jobs, inefficient administration, or unnecessary costs in production. They knew how to mediate conflict between producers when all parties accepted the basic value of economic growth. In creating the Wisconsin Industrial Commission of 1911 — the model for solving industrial relations by regulatory commission — John R. Commons wanted all producers involved in a particular product to organize and to agree among themselves on the most efficient way to create growth. Protected from popular or partisan pressures, the Industrial Commission gave complete freedom to the "leading representatives of conflicting interests" to draft production codes for their industries. Instead of prosecuting employers whose machines injured or killed workers, Commons wanted the state to hire experts in factory safety who would show employers "how to make a profit by preventing accidents."[27]

The dense smoke that billowed from the new factories and apartments was a problem not because it shortened peoples' lives and killed them or because it soiled clothes that hung on lines; it was a problem because it wasted fuel by not consuming it fully before discharging it into the atmosphere. The solution was not to punish the polluter, for that might retard growth, but to teach how to burn coal more efficiently. Regulators like the St. Louis smoke inspector of 1911 wanted to create "a feeling of cooperation between my office and the manufacturers."[28] People who choked as they had to rewash their clothes were experts on how they wanted to live their lives, but to listen to them or to collect their data was potentially to undermine the bureaucratic model at its very core. When people breathed or washed clothes they were not contributing to growth. Consumers had to change their ways to conform to the imperatives for efficient production in the same way that voters and politicians had to abandon their traditional practices to accommodate the reformers' drive for nonpartisan administration.

A final and important part of the process that strengthened the bureaucratic reform tradition at the expense of voters and political parties originated only in part from the reformers, although it was a natural companion to their efforts. Fearing the democratic challenge to corporate values from poorer voters, many leaders successfully promoted reforms that changed the very character of the electorate and its representatives. Over the previous century, politicians had democratized the electorate first by removing the property basis for voting and then, in 1870, removing the racial barrier. Changes of the late nineteenth, and especially the early twentieth, century reversed this democratic trend in four directions. First, some new laws to cover naturalization of immigrants, registration for voting, and voting excluded or intimidated many poor voters.[29] Second, the new commission and manager forms of local government elected on a citywide basis meant, except in a few cases like Seattle, that poor voters would be denied effective representation.[30] Third, reformers enacted measures, particularly in the South, whose sole purpose was to disenfranchise all black and some poor white voters. Administrative reformers in Houston, for example, protected private utilities from public ownership movements only by disenfranchising blacks and poor whites. Poor voters had been the backbone of resistance to the private utility and its allied administrative reformers, but the state poll tax of 1903 at a single stroke cut the poor from 76 percent of Houston's potential electorate to 32 percent.[31] Finally, female suffrage enfranchised the group that Ostrogorski had recognized would be necessary for nonpartisan reform: middle-class women. The net effect of all these changes was to give more votes to the middle class and to disenfranchise poor voters who committed the double sins of supporting partisan politicians and opposing corporate practices.

By weakening the power of political parties to mobilize majorities, the bureaucratic reformers changed the political balance between voters, legislators, and administrators. They replaced the patronage system with the capitalist model of competition. They weakened the power of politicians to manage elections by creating nonpartisan elections. They took the ballot from the traditional supporters of partisan politicians and anticorporate movements and gave it to their enemies. They changed the structures of governments so they were run like corporations and elected in ways that deprived the poor of representation. They created in the independent regulatory commission a system of public administration that was beyond effective control by voters or politicians — a system in which information passed from the top down instead of from the bottom up. In so doing, the bureaucratic reformers succeeded in creating permanent structures that protected the emerging corporations from the perils of universal manhood suffrage far more effectively than the corporations had been able to do with their more direct methods.

THE ANTICORPORATE AND DEMOCRATIC TRADITION

Large-scale industrial capitalism in a political environment of universal manhood suffrage created a second group of reforms whose effect was radically different from the first group, but whose legacy, in the end, was also to weaken traditional political parties and their practices. Equally haunted by the rapid rise of the corporation, these reformers promoted changes that would weaken its political influence and give greater power directly to voters. Because some of these democratic reformers sometimes supported programs of the bureaucratic reformers, because their programs often attracted diverse constituents, and, most important, because they often expressed contempt for politicians, champions of this tradition built less directly on each other's programs than did those of the bureaucratic tradition. The continuity of this tradition was less that of its personnel than that of the common search for political mechanisms that would mobilize potential majorities of voters to control the new corporations better than had the two major political parties.

The democratic reformers derived their vitality from grass roots efforts by citizens to preserve dignity and control over their lives in a world that large corporations were coming increasingly to dominate. Rooted in local traditions, they sought to preserve the value of community against the alien ways that the market increasingly brought to their borders. They resented the growing power of corporations and middlemen and developed their programs from the revolts of traditional cultures. Believing that universal manhood suffrage was the greatest promise in the U.S. political system, they tried to develop new methods to mobilize majorities against new corporate practices. These programs, they hoped, would restore to its original owners, the voters, the power recently taken by corporations. The basic problem was that the corporations seemed increasingly capable of manipulating the political process to gain control of both the Democratic and Republican parties.

As spokespersons for traditional peoples, champions of corporate regulation first believed that political parties were the best way to organize and mobilize democratic reforms. The recent emergence of the Republican Party to supplant the Whigs inspired them to conclude in the 1870s and 1880s that reformers could expect ultimate success by forming third parties to challenge what they considered the unresponsiveness of Democrats and Republicans. From 1880 to 1900 the Greenback-Labor, United Labor, Union Labor, Socialist-Labor, Nationalist, Union Reform, Socialist Democrat, and People's parties all fielded presidential candidates. Even in defeat, third parties were a basic organizing, educating, and mobilizing agency. Since traditional cultures had their sources in local communities, third parties were most appealing to voters in local communities where they reflected particular local patterns of anger at corporate control of politics. In Massachusetts, for example, striking shoeworkers expressed their political anger at shoe manufacturers by victorious Workingmen's Party campaigns in 1878 and 1890 in Lynn, and Social Democratic campaigns in 1898 in Haverhill and in 1899 in Brockton.[32] Milwaukee's workers sent Laborite Henry Smith to Congress in the late 1880s.[33] None of the local third-party campaigns attracted more attention than Henry George's campaigns for mayor of New York in 1886 and 1897. "I see in the gathering enthusiasm" of the city's workers for his independent Labor ticket "a power that is stronger than money," cried George in 1886, "something that will smash the political organizations and scatter them like chaff before the wind."[34]

The quintessential third-party movement derived its vitality from farmers more than from workers. Challenged by an ever-deepening spiral of debt and dependence on private credit lenders such as Southern merchants and Western bankers, farmers banded together in the 1880s to create hundreds of local cooperatives in the farmers' alliance movement. Some three or four million strong, the farmers' alliances were the largest mass movement in the United States during the nineteenth century, and their producer and consumer cooperatives created a vibrant economic and cultural alternative to industrial capitalism. When private bankers and merchants killed the farmers' hopes for a cooperative commonwealth, the alliances entered politics to supplant the private credit system with a public one. After forming local People's parties in 1890, the alliances combined to form a national third party in 1892 as the best hope for escaping the dependence of the major parties on corporations. They gathered at Omaha on July 4, 1892, to declare their independence from the two-party system and from the nonpartisan corporations that controlled both parties:

> We have witnessed for more than a quarter of a century the struggles of the two great political parties for power and plunder, while grievous wrongs have been inflicted upon the suffering people. We charge that the controlling influences dominating both these parties have permitted the existing dreadful conditions to develop without serious effort to prevent or restrain them. They have agreed together to ignore in the coming campaign every issue but one. They propose to drown the outcries of a plundered people with the uproar of a sham battle over the tariff, so that capitalists, corporations, national banks, rings, trusts, watered stock, the demonetization of silver, and the oppressions of the usurers may be lost sight of. They propose to sacrifice our homes, lives and children on the altar of mammon; to destroy the multitude in order to secure the corruption funds from the millionaires.[35]

As they created third parties, campaigned for office, and sometimes won, anticorporate reformers painfully discovered that there were fatal flaws in the structure and traditions not only of political parties but of representative government itself that made third parties an inadequate agency for replacing corporate with democratic control over the economic and political system. The basic problem was that the majority of anticorporate voters created third parties in the hope of enacting specific programs, but the inherent function of a political party is to organize, finance, and win elections. As a result, Populist voters and politicians argued bitterly over whether their most important objective was to win elections, which sometimes meant alliances with a major party, or to preserve their principles. In their eagerness to win the traditional spoils of office, many Populist politicians were willing to betray the movement's voters and their issues by making deals with what Lawrence Goodwyn has brilliantly termed the Populist "shadow movement" in the Democratic Party. "A few leading officials of the People's party by as bald trickery in the way of bossism, bogus proxies, and paper delegates as ever distinguished 'Tammany Hall' assumed supreme control of the party and exercised that control without consulting the popular will and without appeal," charged Davis Waite, Colorado's Populist governor.[36] From Kansas, a Coffey County Populist editor lamented that "what started out as a great uprising of the people for reform, a crusade against evils of which both parties are alike guilty, thus turns out to be a stupendous and perfectly shameless traffic for offices."[37]

The structural imperative of political parties to win elections and distribute spoils even blunted local anticorporate third parties. When shoeworkers and others elected a Workingmen's Party in Lynn, Massachusetts, in both 1878 and 1890, the victorious third party candidates devoted their energies not toward attacking the factory owners whose practices had created the popular drive for the labor party but toward distributing the spoils of office. The party's major victory for workers was the appointment of a more sympathetic police chief — in other words, a simple fulfillment of the old Jacksonian patronage practice.[38]

The election of 1896 demonstrated to many anticorporate reformers the weaknesses of third parties as agencies for organizing and mobilizing mass discontent. When a narrow majority of Populists abandoned their Omaha Platform in 1896 by nominating a Democrat, William Jennings Bryan, in the hope of winning the presidency by combining with a corrupt major party, and when William McKinley's victory in the general election proved that even this compromise strategy was doomed to failure, many reformers gave up hope of organizing anticorporate feeling through political parties. The structures and traditions of political parties made them an ineffective agency to harness sentiments that originated with the spread of large-scale industrial capitalism. Those structures and traditions had evolved before the large corporations, but they had a kind of independent life after the growth of corporations. Not only was it almost impossible to persuade politicians — even those of third parties — that any policy was more important than their own elections and patronage, it was also very difficult to persuade tradition-minded voters to turn against their familiar political parties. The same traditional values that had inspired popular rejection of the new corporate practices also led voters to be extremely reluctant to abandon their ties to older parties that had in the past defended their religious, ethnic, and sectional cultures. The strength of nineteenth-century parties had been their effectiveness in responding to attacks on familiar values by alien ethnoreligious and sectional forces. Their weakness was their persistence in continuing to promote ethnoreligious and sectional politics when industrialization created new kinds of anger of workers, farmers, and consumers.[39]

McKinley's victory in 1896 coincided with a major shift in the grass-roots character of anticorporate attitudes. That shift profoundly influenced the ideologies and programs of democratic reformers in the twentieth century as they sought new political alternatives to organize anticorporate feeling. Beginning on a large scale with the depression of 1893-97, many voters, particularly in cities, concluded that the worst sins of the wealthy and powerful individuals and corporations were those that oppressed them as consumers and taxpayers. This change in the anticorporate tradition represented a change not so much in the objective circumstances of people who opposed corporations, as in the perspective from which they viewed corporate behavior. Where the Populists of the late nineteenth century had created their anticorporate ideology and programs on the hope of uniting citizens who identified with their job and producer roles as farmers and workers, the democratic reformers of the early twentieth century recruited supporters and developed their anticorporate ideology and programs by encouraging people to identify with their common roles and loyalties as consumers and taxpayers regardless of their jobs. The difference was one of perspective and consciousness, not of social or occupational characteristics. The revolt of consumers and taxpayers originated at the local level in protests against death-dealing, expensive, and tax-dodging practices of private utilities in an atmosphere of widespread discontent with the effect of industrial capitalism on traditional values, including the nation's democratic heritage. The spectacular growth of million-dollar corporations, whose capitalization soared from $170 million in 1897 to $20 billion by 1904, produced the first national experience with inflation in the lifetime of most citizens and thereby broadened and deepened the revolt of consumers.

The revolt of consumers and taxpayers had features that shaped the new strategies of democratic reformers. First, consumers and taxpayers were a political majority — the only political majority — and the basic issue was how to translate that majority's views into public policy. Second, consumers and taxpayers had far greater potential for anticorporate action at the local level than at the state and national level because consumption and taxpaying were local acts, rooted in the family, and it was far harder to organize consumers outside their neighborhoods and communities. Third, the structures and traditions of representative government and political parties for nominating and electing candidates and for enacting legislation revolved heavily around corporations, producer groups, and ethnoreligious voters and created enormous problems for consumers and taxpayers.[40]

Champions of consumers and taxpayers developed new political techniques in the democratic reform tradition that aimed to take power from corporations and their political allies and give it instead to voters; that is, to the majority of consumers and taxpayers. Like their anticorporate third-party predecessors, but unlike bureaucratic reformers, democratic reformers were hostile to partisanship only to the extent that it aided corporations in blocking democratic changes. Since consumers and taxpayers had their greatest power at the local level, democratic reformers tried to decentralize policy making. After watching private utilities use political leaders and party discipline in state legislatures to saddle their cities with long-term utility franchises, anticorporate reformers secured a number of changes that took power from state legislators and gave it to voters at the local level. Home rule for cities freed local governments from the death grip of the state legislature. Democratic reformers forced the states to give cities more freedom to acquire public debt that could be used to purchase and build publicly owned utilities. This decentralization of political power was crucial to the success of the most radical and effective program of anticorporate reformers: the movement for municipal ownership. The most widespread socialist experiment in the United States — the municipal ownership movement of this period — was local, not national, and was created by citizens who identified with their roles as consumers and taxpayers, not workers. As part of the drive for public ownership, city governments by 1902 had acquired and converted 170 private electric plants into socialist operations.[41]

When corporations used powerful party leaders or party discipline in legislatures to halt proposals from consumers and taxpayers, democratic reformers sought legislative structural changes that would give more influence over legislation to individual legislators and less to party leaders. They concluded that party leaders used committee assignments, control over access of bills to the floor, campaign contributions, and pork barrel measures to thwart anticorporate legislators and their bills. But the protest against "Czar" Reed and "Cannonsim" in the House of Representatives and "Aldrichism" in the Senate and their counterparts in the state governments was more a protest against corporate control over legislation than against party discipline. Nelson Aldrich's sin during the Payne-Aldrich Tariff debate of 1909 was not that he tried to get all Republicans to vote alike but that he tried to get them to vote against the party's 1908 platform promise, as interpreted by consumers, to lower tariff duties. He was more responsive to nonpartisan corporations than to the party's voters. "What a sardonic jest to speak of [Senate party leaders] as Republicans and Democrats!" cried David Graham Phillips in *The Treason of the Senate*;[42] their treason was bipartisan betrayal of party voters and campaign promises to corporations. Party regularity even under Woodrow Wilson's attempt at parliamentary government never approximated the perfection of strong legislative parties in countries with parliamentary forms of government. As a result, the few legislative changes of this period, such as those promoted by Congressman George W. Norris to weaken the power of the Speaker of the House, were much less significant than attempts to give voters greater influence in selecting candidates and shaping policy.

Betrayed repeatedly by corporation-oriented politicians in both parties, the democratic reformers devoted most of their energies to developing new methods of mobilizing the majority of voters to select candidates and make public policy directly. The Senate, as "the Rich Man's Club," had become the major brake on anticorporate proposals by a familiar process. In years when senators were to be chosen, state legislatures spent their first several weeks in bitter maneuvering, usually amid charges of corporate bribery, to determine who would get the state's biggest patronage plum, the seat in Washington. Legislators rarely chose consumer champions. When democratic reformers stepped up their charges that the Senate reflected corporations first and voters last, charges culminating in the exposure of corporate bribery in the 1909 Illinois legislature when it elected Boss William Lorimer to the Senate, Congress and the states passed a constitutional amendment to give one of the few constitutional prerogatives of state legislatures to the voters instead.

The selection of senators was the tip of the pyramid for selecting public officials that began when a party's voters met first in ward and township caucuses to select delegates to regional and state party conventions that would, in turn, nominate candidates for office. As population growth made candidacies more expensive, and as the growing complexities of economic relationships coupled with more activist governments raised the stakes over those candidacies, corporations came to the aid of aspiring nominees by financing their candidacies at various stages in the nominating process. The convention system of nominations was the cheapest and most efficient way for corporations to control access to public office. Within a single year in Wisconsin, for example, corporations used bribery to prevent democratic reformers from nominating their candidates mayor of Superior and Milwaukee and for governor. Never questioning the potential of political parties to mobilize sympathetic majorities, the democratic reformers solved the problem of corporate control over nominations by giving that power to voters to nominate directly at the polls.

Although party leaders at the time, and political scientists subsequently, lamented that direct primary nominations eroded party government and destroyed the traditional patterns of party responsibility and accountability, democratic reformers believed that this change was the only way that anticorporate majorities could control access to politics and force politicians to honor platform pledges. Wisconsin pioneered the modern, statewide direct primary in 1903, and by 1915 every state was nominating at least some of its candidates by popular vote.[43] The direct primary for delegates to nominate presidents began with several states in 1912.[44] The direct primary gave a great advantage to anticorporate candidates who appealed for the votes of consumers and taxpayers who, in turn, could mobilize their strength in no other way because that strength was their votes, not their formal organization. Even a majority of political scientists polled in 1923 conceded that direct primaries had resulted in candidates who were more responsive to majorities and less to corporations than under the convention system.[45] Believing that the nomination of officeholders was the people's business, not the party's, voters overwhelmingly turned back most campaigns by party leaders to repeal direct primaries. When Nebraska's political leaders repealed the direct primary in the legislature, that state's voters crushingly restored it by direct vote. When legislatures in New York and Idaho repealed their direct primaries, voters turned overwhelmingly to parties that promised to restore the more democratic system.[46] In the early 1940s, three-fourths of Michigan's voters reported that they preferred the direct primary to a restoration of convention nominations.[47]

Voters also demonstrated the democratizing consequences of the direct primary by participating far more heavily in direct primary elections than in earlier caucus elections at the same time that voter turnout in general elections was declining precipitously. In New York, for example, 16 percent of those voting in the general election of 1912 voted in primary caucuses; in the off-year 1914 election — the first direct primary election — that proportion rose to 34 percent.[48] A 10 percent turnout was generally regarded as good in Indiana before the direct primary; the turnout for several years after the direct primary ranged between 50 and 54 percent.[49] Voters obviously nurtured different ideas about responsive and responsible party government than did political leaders who sought to repeal the direct primary.

The most significant of the democratic progressive reforms was not the one that gave to voters the power to nominate but the ones that gave to voters the power to initiate policy directly at the polls without ever having to deal with legislatures or city councils. The initiative and referendum gave to the majority the power to enact measures in the voting booth that had been either rejected or never even considered by legislators. Anticorporate champions of consumer and taxpayer reforms had only to persuade a majority of voters that their measures were desirable. They no longer had even to deal with political parties or leaders. And the initiative and referendum was a direct-outgrowth of the failure of anticorporate third party activity. Stung by the readiness of Populist politicians to behave more like politicians and less like Populists, to betray principle for office, South Dakota's democratic reformers in 1898 enacted the nation's first initiative and referendum measure. Unlike earlier referenda, in which politicians sought popular votes to fulfill constitutional mandates, evade controversial issues, or legitimate new pro-business activities, the initiative process that began in South Dakota gave the initiative over popular votes to voters and reformers to propose measures that they favored. By 1918, it had spread to 22 states and to city governments in even more states.[50] Through the initiative and referendum democratic reformers in the early twentieth century was created a mechanism that, unlike the representative and partisan institutions that survived from preindustrial times, gave some promise of translating popular sentiment into public policy in an industrial society.

The initiative and referendum gave hope to voters who despaired of ever overcoming powerful corporate and political leaders, structures, and traditions. The most militant early promoters of initiative and referendum — Single Taxers, Socialists, and Populists — were those who had concluded that massive redistribution of wealth and power would be more likely to come from direct government than from representative government. Voters became policymakers overnight. In 1909, voters in Denver, Colorado, made policy on 29 issues and in Portland, Oregon, on 35 issues and Oregon's voters became state legislators on 37 issues in 1912. The power to make policy directly, to let majorities rule directly, was very popular. Missouri's voters gave a higher proportion of their votes in 1908 to the proposal for initiative and referendum than for the other seven questions on the ballot that year, and Oregon's voters in 1902 approved it by a 92 percent margin.[51] Voters were so eager for direct government that they were frequently willing to accept whatever went with it. Recognizing this, promoters of commission forms of government tried to gather support for their proposal among poorer voters by including initiative and referendum in their new city charters. Reformer William B. Munro observed in 1912 that the commission plan "would scarcely have met with its present-day favor . . . had its supporters not seized upon the machine of direct legislation and the recall."[52] Although commission government had originated in 1901, it had spread to only 11 cities by 1907. Des Moines, Iowa, sparked the rapid growth of commission government by including direct government for the first time in its commission charter of 1908. In the six years after the Des Moines Plan, 410 cities adopted commission government — and initiative and referendum.[53] Furthermore, voters defended the system of direct policy making even when they rejected the actual measures proposed. Missouri's voters trounced a 1912 initiative that would have enacted the single tax, giving it only 15 percent of their votes, but when enemies of the single tax placed on the 1914 ballot a provision that prohibited Single Taxers from ever using the initiative process in the future, 71 percent of Missouri's votes defended access to the initiative process by Single Taxers.[54]

At the end of this period, many democratic reformers were beginning to suspect that the new administrative bureaucracies would be greater problems than had been elected officials for people who were trying to preserve traditional values. The basic problem with strong administrative agencies was that most citizens believed, in Charles McCarthy's words, that these innovations ran "seemingly contrary to our ideas of democracy."[55] The people were the only real check on special interests and privileged officials. Most citizens profoundly distrusted powerful administrators, whom they tended to equate with George III or the czars of Russia. Many citizens resented experts, powerful bureaucracies, and more remote government. "The people are no longer trusted to manage their own affairs. . . . Real democracy is gone. Bureaucracy has taken its place," lamented T. C. Richmond of Wisconsin in 1914.[56]

As they watched the new bureaucrats perform, many democratic reformers felt confirmed in their traditional fears that bureaucracy was basically a means for protecting privilege. The Ballinger-Pinchot controversy of 1909-10 seemed to prove this as the public and the muckrakers turned a minor squabble between three bureaucrats into a struggle between democracy and privilege. Although Interior Secretary Richard Ballinger was simply administering public land policy in Alaska in keeping with prevailing Western ideas about economic development, most citizens believed he was using administrative discretion to give away billions of dollars worth of valuable national assets to the Morgan and Guggenheim interests. A few years later, in 1914, democratic reformers concluded that the first of the modern regulatory commissions, the Interstate Commerce Commission, reflected the corporate thrust of bureaucracy, its resistance to popular control when it granted the Eastern railroads what the reformers regarded as an unjustified 5 percent rate increase.[57] Local champions of public ownership were furious at the loss of popular control over utilities that accompanied the utility-promoted state regulatory commissions in Wisconsin, New York, California, and Minnesota.[58] The new utility commissions protected the private corporations from public ownership and popular pressures. In Wisconsin, the 1907 legislature, responding to public anger, believed that the railroads controlled the new Railroad Commission and overturned a commission decision setting passenger rates at two and one-half cents a mile, lowering that rate to two cents.[59] In Nebraska, the *Lincoln Daily Star* began a crusade in 1914 to repeal the constitutional amendment that had created that state's railroad commission, because the commission routinely spurned antirailroad complaints.[60] The *Star* agreed with New York Central Railroad President Alfred H. Smith that the state commissions existed mainly to defuse popular anger at railroads.

World War I intervened before democratic reformers could develop mechanisms that would assert popular control over the new administrative agencies that seemed, like all of history's bureaucracies, to be increasingly defending privilege. Reformers realized that it was much harder for legislatures or voters, particularly unorganized consumers, to control corporations once appointed commissions had assumed regulatory powers traditionally reserved to voters and their elected representatives. This was, of course, a major reason why bureaucratic reformers had established them. While legislatures and the initiative process offered occasional opportunities for popular control, democratic reformers groped for more permanent methods. Some of them promoted popular recall of regulatory commissioners, extending a principle some places had applied earlier to judges and city commissioners, thereby holding over regulators the threat of having to account to the public and, it was hoped, making them more responsive to consumers and taxpayers. A second solution, born of frustration with commission decisions, was public ownership, which would, as democratic Mayor Tom L. Johnson of Cleveland observed, give citizens greater control over business decisions in their roles as taxpayers than they had experienced with regulatory commissions in their roles as consumers. After working for 15 years to create responsive regulatory mechanisms for establishing popular control over the railroads, Robert M. La Follette finally concluded that public ownership was the only method that would work.[61] Local champions of utility consumers drew the same conclusion after watching utility regulatory commissions. But the outbreak of World War I prevented the anticorporate reformers from developing as complete methods for democratic control over administrative government as they had created over elected officials. Perhaps the greatest failure of reformers in the years after World War I was their failure to develop mechanisms by which unorganized majorities of voters could directly influence the new administrative agencies created by the bureaucratic reformers. The democratic reforms left a legacy, however incomplete, that weakened the power of party leaders. By taking from legislatures and party leaders and giving to voters the power to elect senators, nominate candidates, and initiate policy, the reformers in this tradition undeniably weakened the accountability of political elites for the activities of party representatives. At the same time, however, the parties achieved a greater responsiveness to wider issues than they had previously had, and more voters participated in nominating candidates than they had before there were direct primaries. Fearing the new powers of voters to make laws directly and to nominate candidates directly, party leaders became more responsive to public opinion and less able to dictate legislation.

THE LEGACY AND THE FUTURE

The "progressive reforms," then, resulted from two radically different, although sometimes overlapping, purposes. Facing the common political reality of universal manhood suffrage, both traditions championed political reforms that would either mobilize or neutralize democratic pressures, that would either advance or retard the growing power of the new large corporations. Both the bureaucratic and democratic reformers sought to change the structures and traditions of politicians and their parties that had evolved in a preindustrial and precorporate environment, and both could point to achievements. As a result of those achievements, these two groups created the two basic challenges to politicians and parties that have persisted to the present. Political leaders lost to voters a considerable amount of power and responsibility for mobilizing voters and making policy, on the one hand, and to nonpartisan administrative government on the other.

The most remarkable thing about the legacy of both reform movements is not what happened, but what did not happen. In contrast to other industrializing countries, where industrial capitalism spawned political parties based more on class and ideological differences, the U.S. political system continued to hinge, as it always had, on competition between candidates of two nonideological parties for office and, in a broad sense, its spoils. In the United States, poor voters (who would have formed class parties in Europe) either disappeared from the electorate during this period or they voted their traditional loyalties.[62] In this sense, both traditions of progressive reformers missed the most significant thing about the relationship of voters to parties. In trying either to limit or extend the power of voters, both groups assumed that parties were potentially at least a vehicle to mobilize popular attitudes toward the new corporations. And in one way they were right. A larger proportion of U.S. workers voted Democratic in the late twentieth century than British workers voted Labour. But the plain truth is that parties were irrelevant and neutral toward the new corporations because they had traditionally mobilized voters along ethnoreligious lines and because the alienation of U.S. workers was circumscribed by ethnoreligious allegiances. Despite a steady increase in the number of voters who styled themselves "independents," the disaffected have failed to develop alternatives to the two-party system for mobilizing voters. The only way that the civil rights or antiwar movements thought to mobilize their growing numbers of supporters within the political process was to support candidates for office in one of the parties. "Who are you going to support?" remains the only question that matters.

At the same time, of course, there is profound popular distrust and dissatisfaction with the performance of politicians and political parties. The parties rank among the most unpopular of U.S. institutions.

Some political thinkers, from Thomas Jefferson to Mao, have suggested that the best way to break up the natural rigidity of governments, to make them more responsive to popular sentiment, is through revolutions, cultural or otherwise. In the United States, at least, the problem stemmed from the fact that representative government and political parties were highly developed before the widespread evolution of industrial capitalism. Voters expressed their anticorporate sentiments only by nominating and electing representatives. Politicians adapted to the anticorporate mood by vaguely promising that if they were elected they would bust trusts or reform taxes. But those who sought to mobilize the majority by either third-party methods or direct-voter nominations soon ran up against the basic fact that representative government created political leaders whose major concern was to win elections, not to translate popular sentiment into policy. They also learned that representative government was far more responsive to organized producers and their campaign contributions than to unorganized majorities of consumers and taxpayers.

The problem with solutions that have been proposed since World War I, whether revolution or further reform of the nominating process, is that they are no longer rooted in the fundamental conviction of the democratic progressives that people are the best judges of what is best for them and that the wisdom of the majority is the wisdom that should prevail. Many U.S. citizens, particularly scholars and political leaders, fundamentally believe that the majority is silent, stupid, conservative, radical, irrational, apathetic, and certainly unstable. But if the basic problem is to create solutions that will allow the majority to get its sentiments acted upon, the starting place must be that of democratic progressives like Lincoln Steffens:

> Uninformed and misinformed; pauperized or over-worked; misled or betrayed by their leaders − financial, industrial, political and ecclesiastical − the people are suspicious, weary, and very, very busy, but they are, none the less, the first, last, and best appeal in all great human cases. Certainly the first rule for the political reformer is: Go to the voters. And the reason seems to be, not that the people are better than their betters, but that they are disinterested; they are not possessed by possession; they have not so many "things" and "friends." They can afford, they are free to be fair. And, though each individual in the great crowd lacks some virtues, they all together have what no individual has, a combination of all the virtues.[63]

The democratic progressives left one legacy that still operates, uniquely, to translate majority sentiment into policy. This is the system of initiative elections, which basically fulfills the heart of Moisei Ostrogorski's proposal for single-interest parties that would free voters to move from issue to issue without corporate or partisan intimidation. Knowing only that voters are unhappy with their practices, politicians in the 1970s have been forced to develop new approaches as a result of initiative elections on proposals like

1978's Proposition 13 in California and 1976's Proposition 1 in Missouri. In Missouri, where corporate-oriented and partisan structures and traditions dominate the legislature, most of the important issues have been settled by popular vote. The unorganized majority, which could find no effective way to overcome special-interest and partisan control over the legislature, used initiatives the past five years to require politicians to divulge sources of campaign funds (a proposal that had never got out of committee); to overturn a Public Service Commission ruling that permitted private utilities to charge consumers in advance for costs of new construction (another proposal that never reached a floor vote); to block the Army Corps of Engineers from damming a free-flowing Ozark river (a proposal rejected by the state's political elite); to pay a special tax that would give the Conservation Department more funds than any other state to acquire land for natural and recreational purposes (a proposal that particularly rankled politicians since they have resented the Conservation Department's unique relationship with voters that goes back to a 1936 initiative election in which voters freed the department from legislative control); to defeat a proposal to exempt certain products from the sales tax because the resulting loss of revenue would curtail public services; and, finally, in 1978, to reject decisively a big-business initiative that would have made Missouri a "right-to-work" state. In Columbia, after the city council had twice defeated the plan, voters enacted a mandatory beverage container deposit ordinance. Special interests, of course, spent millions of dollars to persuade voters, but the voters rejected all of the expensive campaigns. The use of initiatives in Missouri has created the government by discussion that Ostrogorski proposed as an alternative to partisanship, an alternative that has mobilized otherwise apolitical voters to participate in politics with greater intensity than that of the voter who simply casts ballot for party. It has also stimulated countless efforts by politicians to limit its operation.

Initiatives have freed voters to form constantly changing majorities around particular issues. Despite all the structural attacks on partisanship by reformers of the Progressive Era, Missouri politicians could continue to rely on voters to vote straight tickets at general elections. In 1920, the percentage of voters favoring Democratic candidates for ten statewide-elected offices ranged from a low of 43 percent to a high of 44 percent. At the same election, the percentage of voters favoring policy issues on the ballot ranged from 44 percent to 61 percent.[64] Missouri's voters felt far freer of the constraints of traditional partisanship when they faced a choice of issues than when they faced a choice of candidates by major parties.

The initiative process is as popular today as it was in the Progressive Era. In the late 1970s, the Gallup poll found that voters favored a system of national initiative elections by nearly a three-to-one margin.[65] As they have become increasingly frustrated by politicians, more and more groups have used initiatives. For the first time since its inception three-quarters of a century ago, voters are sometimes voting in greater numbers for initiated measures than for candidates when both appear on the same ballot. The most spectacular example was the California primary election of June 1978 when 6.5 million people voted on Proposition 13 and only 5.7 million voted in the gubernatorial primary.[66] Hints of the same phenomenon exist elsewhere. In the Columbia, Missouri, municipal election of 1977, 200 more people voted on the initiative for mandatory beverage container deposits than voted for mayor; in the 1976 general election, more voters in several Missouri counties voted on an anti-utility initiative than voted for governor.

The initiative process has vigorous critics among political leaders and political scientists. At heart, these critics do not respect the voter's ability to understand issues. In a highly influential study of direct government, for example, Clarence Stone concluded that voters understood issues "only in simple and superficial ways," and another study concluded that "ordinary people do not think much about [ballot issues] at all."[67] The basic problem is that such ideas are completely divorced from popular attitudes.

The democratic progressives threw down a challenge to both political parties and administrative bureaucracies that has been only partially fulfilled. That challenge, which ought to lie behind any debate over strong or weak parties, is to create the best system for translating majority sentiment into public policy. The single best alternative at the moment is to amend the Constitution to create an easily accessible system of direct government by voters. The cure for the evils of democracy is now, as ever, more democracy.

NOTES

1. Karl Marx, *Capital,* trans. Ben Fowkes, ed. Ernest Mandel (New York: Vintage Books, paperback ed., 1977), I, p. 397, for example, and Engels, *The Condition of the Working Class in England* (1845; London: Panther Books, paperback ed., 1969), esp. pp. 254-262. Edward P. Thompson, *The Making of the English Working Class* (1963; New York: Vintage Giant, paperback ed.) is the seminal neo-Marxist interpretation and on p. 826 he makes the point explicit.

2. *Democracy and the Organization of Political Parties,* vol. II, *The United States* (Garden City: Anchor Books, paperback ed., 1964).

3. Charles A. Beard, *An Economic Interpretation of the Constitution of the United States* (New York: Macmillan, 1913); J. Allen Smith, *The Spirit of American Government* (New York: Macmillan, 1907).

4. Henry George, "Money in Elections," *North American Review* 136 (March 1883): 201-11.

5. M. Ostrogorski, *Democracy and the Organization of Parties,* II, 95-101, for example.

6. The effect of Granger legislation in driving businessmen to seek more direct methods of controlling political parties can be traced for Wisconsin in

E. Bruce Thompson, *Matthew Hale Carpenter, Webster of the West* (Madison: State Historical Society of Wisconsin, 1954), pp. 221, 225-30, 231-32; Graham A. Cosmas, "The Democracy in Search of Issues: The Wisconsin Reform Party, 1873-1877," *Wisconsin Magazine of History* 46 (Winter 1962-63): 97, 108; Richard W. Hantke, "Elisha W. Keyes, the Bismarck of Western Politics," *Wisconsin Magazine of History* 31 (September 1947): 29-41; Herman J. Deutsch, "Railroad Politics," *Wisconsin Magazine of History* 15 (June 1932): 391-411; and William L. Burton, "The First Wisconsin Railroad Commission: Reform or Political Expediency?" (M. S. thesis, University of Wisconsin, 1952).

7. Matthew Josephson, *The Politicos, 1865-1896* (New York: Harvest, paperback ed., 1963), p. 406, for example.

8. David P. Thelen, *The New Citizenship: Origins of Progressivism in Wisconsin, 1885-1900* (Columbia: University of Missouri Press, 1972), pp. 28-31, 250-289, and Clay McShane, *Technology and Reform: Street Railways and the Growth of Milwaukee, 1887-1900* (Madison: State Historical Society of Wisconsin, 1974), p. 117, trace this process in Milwaukee politics.

9. See, for example, Lincoln Steffens, *The Shame of the Cities* (New York: American Century, paperback ed., 1957), pp. 69-100, and Walton Bean, *Boss Ruef's San Francisco* (Berkeley and Los Angeles: University of California Press, paperback ed., 1968).

10. Matthew Josephson, *The Robber Barons: The Great American Capitalists, 1861-1901* (New York: Havest, paperback ed., 1962), p. 132.

11. Thelen, *New Citizenship*, p. 255.

12. For example, see Thelen, *New Citizenship*, pp. 138-141, and Martin J. Schiesl, *The Politics of Efficiency: Municipal Administration and Reform in America, 1880-1920* (Berkeley: University of California Press, 1977), chapters 2 and 3.

13. Thelen, *New Citizenship*, p. 141.

14. Victor J. West, "The California Direct Primary," *Annals of the American Academy of Political and Social Science* 106 (March 1923): 116-17.

15. Robert Eugene Cushman, "Non-Partisan Nominations and Elections," ibid., pp. 83-96.

16. Schiesl, *Politics of Efficiency*, pp. 51-54.

17. The literature on this subject is rich and voluminous. See, for examples, Jerald Elliot Levine, "Police Parties, and Polity: The Bureaucratization, Unionization and Professionalization of the New York City Police, 1870-1917" (Ph.D. dissertation, University of Wisconsin, 1971), and John F. Bauman, "Disinfecting the Industrial City: The Philadelphia Housing Commission and Scientific Efficiency, 1909-1916," in *The Age of Urban Reform: New Perspectives on the Progressive Era*, ed. Michael Ebner and Eugene M. Tobin (Port Washington, N.Y.: Kennikat Press, 1977), 117-130.

18. Statistics on commission forms are in Bradley Robert Rice, *Progressive Cities: The Commission Government Movement in America, 1901-1920* (Austin: University of Texas Press, 1977), pp. 113-25, and on manager forms in Inter-

national City Managers' Association, *The Municipal Year Book: 1934,* p. 92. The statistics on government forms in 1933 are from *The Municipal Year Book: 1934,* pp. 107-110. Richard S. Childs, chief proponent of city manager government, explains why commission government gave way to manager forms in his book, *The First 50 Years of the Council-Manager Plan of Municipal Government* (New York: National Municipal League, 1965), esp. pp. 76-78.

19. Frederick W. Taylor, *The Principles of Scientific Management* (New York: Norton Library, paperback ed., 1967), p. 36.

20. Schiesl, *Politics of Efficiency,* p. 112.

21. Ibid., pp. 112-122, 131.

22. Kenneth Fox, *Better City Government: Innovation in American Urban Politics, 1850-1937* (Philadelphia: Temple University Press, 1977), pp. 63-89, explores the effect of the Census Bureau model.

23. Although Kolko's major argument in both *Triumph of Conservatism* (New York: Free Press of Glencoe, 1963) and *Railroads and Regulation* (Princeton, N.J.: Princeton University Press, 1965) is that corporations created the federal commissions to solve competitive problems, he provides numerous examples to support the point, particularly for railroads, that more radical and democratic forces were also pushing for regulation and taxation.

24. Marver Bernstein, *Regulating Business by Independent Commission* (Princeton, N.J.: Princeton University Press, 1955).

25. Charles McCarthy, *The Wisconsin Idea* (New York: Macmillan, 1912), p. 177.

26. Ibid., p. 289.

27. John R. Commons, *Myself: The Autobiography of John R. Commons* (Madison: University of Wisconsin Press, paperback ed., 1964), p. 157.

28. R. Dale Grinder traces these conflicts in "The Anti Smoke Crusades: Early Attempts to Reform the Urban Environment, 1893-1918" (Ph.D. diss., University of Missouri, 1973).

29. Robert D. Marcus, *Grand Old Party: Political Structure in the Gilded Age, 1880-1896* (New York: Oxford University Press, 1971), p. 253.

30. Samuel P. Hays, "The Politics of Reform in Municipal Government in the Progressive Era," *Pacific Northwest Quarterly* 55 (October 1964): 157-69; James Weinstein, "Organized Business and the City Commission and Manager Movements," *Journal of Southern History* 28 (May 1962): 166-82; Edward J. Kopf, "The Environments of Reform: Economics, Culture, and the Chelsea Board of Control, 1908-1914," in *Age of Urban Reform,* ed. Ebner and Tobin, pp. 13-27.

31. Harold L. Platt, "City-Building and Progressive Reform: The Modernization of an Urban Polity: Houston, 1892-1905," ibid., pp. 28-42.

32. Alan Dawley, *Class and Community: The Industrial Revolution in Lynn* (Cambridge: Harvard University Press, 1976), chapter 8; Henry F. Bedford, *Socialism and the Workers in Massachusetts, 1886-1912* (Amherst: University of Massachusetts Press, 1966), chapters 3 and 4.

33. Thelen, *New Citizenship,* pp. 25-26, 42-43.

34. Edmund Morris, *The Rise of Theodore Roosevelt* (New York: Coward, McCann and Geoghegan, 1979), p. 344.

35. The Omaha Platform as reprinted in Norman Pollack, ed., *The Populist Mind* (Indianapolis: Bobbs-Merrill, paperback, 1967), p. 61. This account of Populism is based on Lawrence Goodwyn, *Democratic Promise: The Populist Movement in America* (New York: Oxford University Press, 1976); Peter H. Argersinger, *Populism and Politics: William Alfred Peffer and the People's Party* (Lexington: University Press of Kentucky, 1974); and C. Vann Woodward, *Origins of the New South, 1877-1913* (Baton Rouge: Louisiana State University Press, 1951).

36. Argersinger, *Populism and Politics,* p. 307.

37. Ibid., p. 141.

38. Dawley, *Class and Community,* chapter 8.

39. The central role of ethnoreligious attitudes in shaping nineteenth century partisanship can be traced in Lee Benson, *The Concept of Jacksonian Democracy: New York as a Test Case* (New York: Atheneum Books, paperback ed., 1964); Ronald P. Formisano, *The Birth of Mass Political Parties: Michigan, 1827-1861* (Princeton, N.J.: Princeton University Press, 1971); Paul Kleppner, *The Cross of Culture: A Social Analysis of Midwestern Politics, 1850-1900* (New York: Free Press, 1970); Richard Jensen, *The Winning of the Midwest: Social and Political Conflict, 1888-1896* (Chicago: University of Chicago Press, 1971), for examples.

40. This interpretation follows Thelen, *New Citizenship,* and Thelen, *Robert M. La Follette and the Insurgent Spirit* (Boston: Little, Brown, 1976).

41. Commission on Public Ownership and Operation, National Civic Federation, *Municipal and Private Operation of Public Utilities* (New York: National Civic Federation, 1907), I, 162.

42. Phillips, *The Treason of the Senate* (1906: Chicago: Quadrangle Books, paperback ed., 1964), p. 93. David J. Rothman, *Politics and Power: The United States Senate, 1869-1901* (Cambridge: Harvard University Press, 1966) misinterprets the movement for direct election of senators as an attack on partisanship.

43. Ernest S. Griffith, *A History of American City Government: The Progressive Years and Their Aftermath, 1900-1920* (New York: Praeger, 1974), pp. 71-73.

44. Thelen, *La Follette and Insurgent Spirit,* chapter 5, suggests a sharp conflict between the new presidential primaries and the politicians' traditional motives in 1912.

45. William E. Hannan, "Opinions of Public Men on the Value of the Direct Primary," *Annals* 106 (March 1923): 57.

46. George W. Norris, "Why I believe in the Direct Primary," ibid., p. 29.

47. James K. Pollock, *The Direct Primary in Michigan, 1909-1935* (Ann Arbor: University of Michigan Press, 1943), p. 70.

48. Louise Overacker, "The Operation of the State-Wide Direct Primary in New York State," *Annals* 106 (March 1923): 145.

49. Frederick H. Guild, "The Operation of the Direct Primary in Indiana," ibid., p. 172.

50. Austin Ranney, "United States of America," in *Referendums: A Comparative Study of Practice and Theory,* ed. Austin Ranney and David Butler (Washington, D.C.: American Enterprise Institute for Public Policy Research, 1978), p. 70.

51. *Official Manual of the State of Missouri for the Years 1909-1910,* p. 810.

52. Quoted in Rice, *Progressive Cities,* p. 72.

53. The crucial addition of direct government can be traced in ibid., pp. 34-51, 72-83, and in Tso-Shuen Chang, *History and Analysis of the Commission and City-Manager Plans of Municipal Government in the United States* (Iowa City: University of Iowa Press, 1918), p. 75-96.

54. Norman L. Crockett, "The 1912 Single Tax Campaign in Missouri," *Missouri Historical Review* 56 (October 1961): 40-52.

55. McCarthy, *Wisconsin Idea,* p. 177.

56. Quoted in Herbert F. Margulies, *The Decline of the Progressive Movement in Wisconsin, 1890-1920* (Madison: State Historical Society of Wisconsin, 1968), p. 147.

57. Thelen, *La Follette and Insurgent Spirit,* 74-76, 114-115.

58. For example, S. P. Jones to Robert M. La Follette, April 9, 1913, La Follette Papers, Manuscripts Division, Library of Congress.

59. Stanley P. Caine, *The Myth of a Progressive Reform: Railroad Regulation in Wisconsin, 1903-1910* (Madison: State Historical Society of Wisconsin, 1970), p. 167.

60. *Lincoln Daily Star,* February 9, 1914, clipping enclosed in E. E. Wolfe to Robert M. La Follette, February 9, 1914, La Follette Papers.

61. Thelen, *La Follette and Insurgent Spirit,* pp. 114-17.

62. Marcus, *Grand Old Party,* pp. 255-56.

63. Lincoln Steffens, *Upbuilders* (Seattle: University of Washington Press, paperback ed., 1968), p. xi.

64. State of Missouri, *Official Manual, 1921-22,* 298-309, 468-477.

65. Ranney, "The United States," p. 75.

66. Eugene C. Lee, "California," in Ranney and Butler, *Referendums,* p. 108.

67. Clarence Stone, "Local Referendums: An Alternative to the Alienated Voter Model," *Public Opinion Quarterly* 29 (Summer 1965): 219; Bertil L. Hanson, "Oklahoma's Experience with Direct Legislation," *Southwestern Social Science Quarterly* 47 (December 1966): 273.

DISCUSSION OF THE THELEN ESSAY

James MacGregor Burns

David Thelen's paper raises this question in my mind. There seems to be an element of volition, an element of choice, of planning, of deliberate design, on the part of the main actors or leadership groups with which you deal. I wonder how you go about this. When you argue that they were trying to do such and such, to what extent can you go into a kind of motivational or rationalistic analysis? How do you accumulate data that indicate to you this was their plan as against some other plan, considering the fact that many untoward events often come out of these various plans?

David Thelen

I agree that events often forced the actors to change and modify their proposals as they discovered problems with earlier solutions. But those changes occurred within frameworks bounded by ideologies, procedures, and constituents. Some actors explained very clearly why they wanted particular changes, and you can determine intent from their explanations. In the case of independent regulatory commissions, for example, the personality and values of Thomas Cooley, the first head of the first commission, the Interstate Commerce Commission, clearly set the basic pattern for later commissions. Cooley wanted to protect corporations from excessive public or governmental regulation, and he devised the semijudicial approach, instead of others that would have encouraged greater public participation. You can also detect the basic thrust of a proposal by looking at which groups supported and opposed it and their reasons. Labor, tax reform, socialist, and Populist groups generally favored direct democracy, for example. Champions of consumers, from the Progressive Era to Ralph Nader, have generally criticized the procedures and decisions of regulatory commissions more than have representatives of producers.

Gerald Pomper

I want to raise a number of questions. The increase in the number of primary election participants does not in itself prove to me that primary voters are more representative of the mass electorate than people who participated in caucuses. I also doubt whether evidence of the past five years of Missouri initiatives and referenda tells us much about the effect of progressive reforms. Further, I doubt that a variation in the vote on one side or the other necessarily tells us anything significant. Those are data questions.

More fundamentally, I question the premise that the initiative is inherently a more democratic device than party participation. This argument misses the qualitative component of democratic participation. Participation in initiatives, referenda, and primaries is a sporadic, isolated, noncommunitarian form of participation. By its very nature, this is an individual act which has much less basis in a democratic community than involvement in organizations such as political parties.

You take voting on initiatives as an exemplar of greater democratic participation. It may be. However, I would argue that in terms of a democratic community which is based on discussion, interaction, and some sense of coherence, it is less than exemplary.

To go further, the development of the initiative might better be viewed as increase in the bureaucratization of society, rather than as a counter to it. If you think of bureaucratization as increasing specialization, giving more things to experts, you can see an extension of that in the initiative. One would have experts making policy and then, once in a while, you consult the broad electorate.

Indeed, some of the ideologies supporting the city manager system even spoke in these terms. Using the analogy of the corporation, there is a board of directors who are expert and then every so often the directors go back to the stockholders for their views, their ratification, and occasionally their intervention. So what you call the democratic thrust is not opposite to the bureaucratic thrust; in many ways it is along the same lines.

My final point is historical. That is the old point about the latent functions of reform. Even if the intentions of the second group of progressives were as you have pictured them, it seems to me the effects of their reforms have not been in the direction they intended. For example, there was the revolt against Speaker Cannon. You say that was in the interest of democratization. So it was claimed to be at the time, but the result was to fracture power and make it more accessible to special interests, rather than less accessible, because of the development of the committee system and strong deference to seniority. The purpose of the direct primary was certainly democratization, but the effect in many ways has been to leave elections more vulnerable to small groups. The purpose of the initiative is also democratization. The effect, as we know from a great deal of research, is to give power to those who have more wealth and more access to advertising and to the mass media. The initiative and referendum are not instruments of broad, popular mass movements.

Whatever the progressives' intentions, the effect has been not to build a democratic community but to build the increasingly isolated, fractured non-community that we see in the United States.

David Thelen

Beginning with small points, I certainly think that commission and manager governments were bureaucratic, not democratic. The point is that the bureaucratic reforms in local government structures never would have spread if the people who were promoting them had not linked them to direct democracy. Supporters of direct democracy accepted commission and manager governments only because they were the easiest way to get initiative and referendum on the local level. In the grass roots debates over these new city charters, few champions of direct democracy made the connection you do — expert rule with occasional plebiscites. In fact, some scholars like Clarence Stone wrongly generalize about the plebiscitarian role of direct democracy by looking at all popular votes, many of which were indeed initiated by leaders and experts, instead of looking at initiative elections. Initiative elections are difficult and expensive processes that people resort to only after legislatures or regulatory commissions — leaders, experts, if you like — have rejected their causes.

I don't agree with you that parties are more participatory and communitarian than initiative campaigns. First of all, most people participate in either initiative or candidate elections simply by voting. Second, groups promoting particular ballot initiatives raise funds, recruit participants, and spread the gospel in ways that are similar to those of the parties. The difference is whether the participants are committed to causes or to spoils in a broad sense. Promoters of initiatives have been committed solely to victory at the polls while there have been many times and places where party leaders have been willing to lose elections in order to maintain their control over party machinery. Parties, in theory, should be more participatory because they have had greater continuity than initiative-oriented groups, but during the Progressive Era this was not always even true. Groups like the Single-Taxers and Oregon's People's Power League lasted longer than the dominant factions in several statewide parties in the Progressive Era. The notion of parties as broadly democratic, communitarian, and participatory strikes me as a noble dream, but not the reality in the United States. I guess our difference comes down to my agreement with Ostrogorski's comment about the functioning of political parties and his solution that the problems of political parties are best resolved by some sort of discussion process and that something like single-interest parties or the initiative is probably the best way to accomplish that.*

I agree with you that initiatives have not accomplished all the goals of their initial enthusiasts and that some democratic changes, like the weakening of the Speaker's powers, have actually led to changes that have made government less responsive. But the solution is not to wish the change had never occurred, but to improve on it.

---

*I. Ostrogorski, *Democracy and the Organization of Political Parties,* 2 vols., Frederick Clarke, trans. (New York: Macmillan, 1902).

Democratic progressives recognized the problem that both sides of an initiative might not have equal access to public opinion. They solved it in many states by publishing handbooks that gave both sides the opportunity to make their cases. The solution today might be to require all sides to an issue to have the same amount of access to the forums of discussion such as television and radio. If it were not unconstitutional, you could also limit the amount that one side could spend. The democratic reform tradition has been more vital in advancing reforms of nominations than of initiatives.

Austin Ranney

It is well to remember that we are dealing here with one of the great watersheds in the history of American parties. Prior to the Progressive Era, American parties at both the national and the subnational levels were quite similar to their counterparts in England. For example, Ostrogorski's description of the Birmingham caucus of Joe Chamberlain was quite similar to descriptions of urban machines in the United States.

However, when we adopted the direct primary, we made our party system unlike any other in the world. Even today, no other nation in the world uses the direct primary. On a few occasions a few countries use something that looks a bit like it, but the difference is that the participants in those pseudoprimaries are dues-paying, card-carrying party members, and not anybody who merely names himself a party member as is the case in the United States.

It strikes me that when we discuss the Progressive Era, we deal with issues and problems that are still with us today. Many of the party reforms made since 1968 have sought the same goals the progressives sought. The basic objective of both sets of reformers was to minimize the role of intermediary institutions. The progressives believed that the basic cause for the deficiencies of the political system was the self-selected go-between agencies such as the parties and the corporations, which had insinuated themselves between the sovereign people and their government. So the remedy was obvious: Sweep those agencies out of the way or bypass them. Take the power to make nominations away from the bosses in the smoke-filled rooms and give it to the people directly. Make laws not by filtering ideas through a corrupt and compromising legislature but by direct popular action through initiatives and referendums.

Judging by the public opinion polls, the most popular reforms today reflect the same basic ideas. For example, about 70 percent of the people favor nominating presidential candidates by one-day national primaries, rather than by national party conventions. About the same proportion favor abolishing the electoral college in favor of direct election of the president without regard to state lines. And there is about the same support for a national initiative and referendum. So perhaps the Progressive Era was the true seed time for our contemporary ideas about parties and other intermediary institutions.

Richard McCormick

I would like to pick up on that and make it a bit more explicit because I think it gets to the heart of the enormous issue that is presented by the paper today.

It is the issue of confidence in representative government versus confidence in direct democracy. We started out in the 1780s not only with a strong expressed confidence in representative government but an equally strongly expressed lack of confidence in direct democracy.

It seemed in the early period, down to the 1830s, that we might as a people be prepared to accord a certain autonomy to government. This is noticeable particularly at the state level. State constitutions reposed virtually unlimited authority in state governments and particularly in state legislatures.

Then between the 1830s and the 1870s what is perhaps the most significant change that has ever occurred in the American political system took place. In a series of constitutional conventions between the 1830s and the 1870s, not only were restraints placed upon state legislatures — very serious restraints — but we also got the beginnings of direct democracy, which I gather Professor Thelen finds emerging in the twentieth century.

State constitutional conventions, as we know, wrote laws into constitutions. Not only that, they eased the amending process, with the consequence that significant matters of policy were increasingly determined not be representative institutions but by referenda in the form of constitutional amendments.

What we had taking place between the 1830s and the 1870s is what Willard Hurst has called a denial of autonomy to government. In another sense, it represented on the part of the American people a vote of lessened confidence, if not no confidence, in representative government, and the insistence upon withdrawing more and more power not simply from the legislatures but from all governmental institutions at the state level, and reserving those powers to the people. I could develop that a bit further, but I want to come back to the point of strong and weak parties.

It seems to me that closely related to the question of strong and weak parties is the question of strong and weak government. I would be prepared to argue, although I will not take the time to try to do it now, that the massive change that took place in the American political system at the state level between the 1830s and the 1870s represented a strong emergence of the view that the American people did not want strong government in the sense of according autonomy to representative institutions. By the same token, I think the whole history of American parties suggests that the American people have never wanted strong political parties for the same reasons, essentially, that they have not wanted strong government.

This whole issue of strong versus weak parties must be associated with the issue of strong versus weak government. As I understand the political traditions of the American people, we are a people to whom democracy means liberty more than it means governance. This has a very direct relationship to the whole large issue before us today of strong and weak parties and strong and weak government.

Lee Benson

I want to raise one theoretical question and then pose two specific questions. It seems to me the central issue of the conference might be put in this fashion: Can there be democratic, participatory, strong parties that produce strong, effective, and democratic government? That seems to me to be the central issue. Instead of debating it theoretically, however, I would like to ask Professor Thelen two empirical questions.

Do you think that the American governmental system functioned more effectively and more democratically between 1902 and 1916 than it had between 1870 and 1902? Is there a strong, positive relationship between the various progressive movements and the relative differences in the functioning of the American governmental system between 1902 and 1916 compared to its functioning between 1870 and 1902?

To make the questions clearer, I would argue that after 1900, the governmental system functioned much more effectively than it had before. There was indeed a strong, positive relationship not with any one of the particular "reforms" but with the basic thrust of transforming the political and party systems as they had existed prior to 1902.

David Thelen

Is the operative word "effective"?

Lee Benson

"Effective government." I might as well disagree with my friend, Richard McCormick, on this. I think liberty versus effectiveness is a false dichotomy. In fact, given the ethos of American society, it is indispensable to have liberty, democracy, *and* effective government. Unless we have all three, we are not going to have any of them. That is my basic argument. Posing the problem in the fashion of either liberty or effective government poses a contradiction which I do not believe exists in fact.

However, my question is this: Did the governmental system work better between 1902 and 1916 in terms of realizing certain values such as increasing the quality of life — better in a whole set of specific ways which everyone would agree were desirable?

David Thelen

I guess my question is: Effective for whom?

Lee Benson

That is what I am asking you. Did it work better for the "mass" of the American people? Did it work better particularly for the disadvantaged groups in society or those groups which had relatively little influence on government decisions in the pre-1900 period? Were they responsible for the changes in government or not? Did they benefit from the programs of government at national, state, and local levels?

Arthur Link

I think the question that Lee Benson has raised is a key question, a crucial one. Here one can speak only generally, with perhaps a few particulars.

I think we all know that in 1901, the government of the United States — I am talking about the national government, and I am going to stick with that — was securely controlled by not more than eight or ten persons in the Senate and three or four in the House of Representatives. It can be demonstrated that there simply was no correlation between political leadership at that level and the mass of people. It can be equally demonstrated that by 1918 or 1919, government had become not only more efficient but, much more important, that instrumentalities had been created and were in fact operating for the benefit of much broader constituencies. I will not say the whole country. I am not talking about a paradise. There were, and always are going to be, disadvantaged groups.

There are dozens of examples. Let's take tax policy. In 1900, there was no tax on wealth except for local and state taxes. In 1913, a small income tax was imposed. In 1916, the highest income tax ever enacted in peacetime by any country up to that time was enacted. Moreover, the effect of the very high tax system during 1917-18, when the country was at war, was to decrease greatly the share of wealthy people and to increase the share of workers and farmers. That is one illustration.

Let us take antitrust policy as another example. I used to think that it was inconsequential, but I have changed my mind. I have been convinced by the authorities in this field that there is no question that the movement toward "trustification" and "cartelization" from 1901 to 1921 was reversed by a very vigorous antitrust policy. I could give you details, but I will not go into them.

Or take the whole question of access to credit. Very few people had access to credit in 1900. The Federal Reserve System opened up credit to small consumers, the Federal Farm Loan Act of 1916 broadened it, and so on.

I cannot see how there could be much disagreement on the fact that, by 1928, the government of the United States was vastly more responsive to masses of people — and I do not mean just the middle class — than it had been in 1900 or 1901. 1900 was a millionaire's paradise in this country.

David Thelen

I agree with Professor Benson that the democratic reforms of the Progressive Era generally created more responsive and democratic parties and more responsive and democratic government than had existed before 1900. Competition within parties, for example, was much less likely to be the nineteenth century struggle between ins and outs and much more likely to be based on differences over issues. Whether one looks at Wisconsin or California Republicans or Georgia or Texas Democrats, the most striking impact of the direct primary, it seems to me, was to turn traditional party factionalism into ideological factionalism. As a result of giving voters power to nominate candidates and make policy, state and national governments enacted measures that were more responsive to the "mass" of voters than in the last of the nineteenth century.

Looking at the political changes in that period from the vantage point of direct democracy, however, I am struck that the gains made by producers groups (labor and farm organizations, for example) were significantly greater at the state and national levels than those made by consumers and taxpayers. The most effective response to the challenge of the large-scale corporation — something we have not talked about yet — came at the local level with municipal ownership by consumers and taxpayers, but the traditions and structures of representative government and political parties made it much harder to develop an equally effective response at the state and national levels, where parties rarely chose to mobilize the consumer revolt of the period. If responsiveness to majority concerns is the criterion for effective government, I feel obliged to suggest that the record of the Progressive Era was less than perfect.

James Banner

Does representative government necessitate parties and does direct democracy exclude them? Depending upon whether the balance swings in favor of representative government or in favor of direct democracy, there may very well be available to us different kinds of party systems under different circumstances. We have to ask ourselves under what circumstances can one measure weakness and strength in party systems. What are the historical, social, and political contexts under which those questions are to be asked and measures developed?

David Thelen

I don't know what conditions are necessary or sufficient, but it does seem that representative government has done a better job of representing organized minorities of all sorts, as perhaps the authors of the *Federalist Papers* had intended, than of representing poorly organized majorities. Because the ballot preceded the large corporation in the United States, I think that representative government in this country will create parties that more dedicated to electing candidates than enacting policies aimed at corporate power — at least as compared with European countries with representatives institutions. I agree with Ostrogorski that direct government will create the kind of issue-oriented "parties" that might be an alternative.

Kay Lawson

I would like to turn around our way of looking at this paper. I found it very interesting and very exciting if we ask not why did the progressives do what they did but why has what they did been maintained? David Thelen's paper demonstrates two separate responses to progressivism. It shows that for some people, identified somewhat simplistically as corporates or corporatists, it offered an opportunity to move in and replace party leadership, take over patronage, and exert control in a way that for a few years they had no doubt feared they were going to lose. They thought: No, we can do it this way instead. So they were instrumental, it would seem, in maintaining some of these reforms.

Thus, instead of implying self-serving motives for the creation of these reforms, we might consider if there were such motives for *maintaining* those reforms. Such a study might help us to move forward. Many of those who have studied the results of the progressive movement have said, "These benighted reformers, these do-gooders, look what they have done to the parties." Yet we have still been afraid to move out and undo what they did, because somehow in the back of our minds we have feared they were right, that strong parties were in themselves dangerous, that any time we have strong parties we will have strong government working on behalf of the interests of a narrow elite. We cannot quite shake loose from that concern, and as long as we cannot we are not free to move away from the progressive changes. But if we recognize that the changes which weakened parties did *not* curb the power of special interests, then perhaps we can begin to say: "All right, let's talk about a new kind of strong party, let's talk about strong parties that really do serve as intermediaries from people to state."

Arthur Link

You are talking about the Democratic party under Woodrow Wilson, as a matter of fact.

Gerald Pomper

The theoretical basis of democracy that you have here is strictly an individualistic one. Decisions are made by philosophical voters and citizens who think individually about what is the public good and go out and vote for it in initiatives or in elections. That is not an attainable conception of democracy.

To borrow a phrase, we might talk about participatory democracy. It involves some kind of interaction, discussion, and organization. However, the tendency of initiatives and direct primaries is to isolate voters, to break them up ultimately into individual cells, rather than to bring them together in a common organization.

If you follow the individualist idea, inevitably you get frustrated. What happens, in fact, to any kind of mass organizations, parties, or others? They decline if they do not have things to do and are less available for social movements. Why do we need organizations? Individuals who are rich and powerful have all kinds of advantages in society. One needs mass organizations in order to overcome those inherent or obtained advantages of the powerful and the rich.

It is consistent. Where you have mass organizations — parties being among the most prominent, although not the only one — you are able to some extent to offset the advantages of wealth, status, and power. Actions which weaken those organizations simply reinforce the power of those who hold power on other grounds, primarily economic.

To ignore these facts and say: "Well, if only people would get themselves together and act in their interests" — that response is no help. It assumes some permanent majority that is constantly being disadvantaged, and there are not too many majorities such as that. Ultimately, it leads to the alienation you talked about. The alienation comes not so much from people not being able to vote in national initiatives but from the policy results being unsatisfactory as the electorate is fractured into more and more single-interest groups.

More basically, the lack of associations which people have, the alienation of American life, is directly due to the extreme individualism. I am not just talking about elections, I am talking about suburbanization, the breakup of the family, and so on. The destruction of party is simply another destruction, and a very vital one, of those critical intermediate associations. I do not see how that promotes any kind of meaningful democracy.

David Thelen

I think that the beauty of the initiative system is that it acknowledges and tries to address the very individualism you are talking about. It provides an intermediary mechanism for mobilizing otherwise unorganized majorities behind a particular program.

Why are political parties less popular than initiatives if they perform their functions in the way you describe? For some reason, political parties have not functioned in the twentieth century as the ideal intermediaries that you and I would desire as a way for the disadvantaged to offset the advantages of the privileged. Texas, for example, would have elected less conservative officials in the last election if poor blacks and latinos in that state's cities had been any reason to participate in the most marginal kind of way in their party's affairs — by simply voting. Are disadvantaged voters turned off by a process in which candidates adopt policies favorable to large and organized campaign contributors rather than to the unorganized or even the less powerful of organized groups? Groups less powerful than corporations, such as organized labor, cannot even get a Democratic Congress and president to support its minor reforms of the organizating process that would unquestionably create intermediary institutions for the disadvantaged when they deal with their employers.

Judson James

Progressives run the educational system. There is a growth in partisan identification up until high school, but a decline following that when you start getting formal civic education in high schools. There are fragments of the official political ideology of educators which show very strong reinforcement of antiparty attitudes in the formal educational process.

You have touched upon one of the most important elements. Fundamentally, we have an individualistic culture which basically will always be hostile to parties. We have to mitigate the effects of that hostile environment to some degree. It is an uphill struggle to convince anybody about parties.

Donald Robinson

Earlier, Professor Thelen was criticized for inadequate concern for liberty and minority rights. My concern is that his paper reflects inadequate concern for popular government. Parties perform an essential function if there is to be popular government; namely, the function of aggregating interests, or prioritizing claims upon the government, deciding which claims to satisfy first.

There are certain things governments have to do. They have to regulate the economy. They have to raise taxes. They have to conduct foreign relations and provide for defense. Governments now have to provide for the general welfare, and protect the environment, and so forth and so on. The government has to do all these things. For this reason, it seems to me, Ostrogorski is not only wrong in suggesting that single-interest parties are the solution, that they would allow voters to move from issue to issue without corporate or partisan intimidation, but his term *single-interest parties* is a misnomer, a contradiction in terms. Parties, at least in the sense in which the term is used in America, cannot concentrate on single issues precisely because parties aggregate.

Ostrogorski was right in something else he said, and we will talk more about this later; namely, that parties and party leaders have interests of their own. Therefore, they must be watched very carefully. They must be kept open to popular participation. The sources of their funds must be watched. Their focus on issues must be maintained. They must not be allowed to degenerate into patronage mills.

Above all, though, it cannot be forgotten by those who care about democracy in this country that parties perform an essential function if popular government is to be achieved. This point was lost to the progressive reformers. I regret to say that it seems to be lost in the argument of this paper.

Lee Benson

I am not sure we can confront the issues that arise in this discussion unless we know what we mean by strong or weak parties. We do not want to go into detailed conceptual definitions, but some conceptual clarity is mandatory. For example, I found myself agreeing with Otis Graham until he said that this was an era of weak parties. My reading of the progressive movements is just the reverse of that. What most progressives wanted was strong parties to achieve progressive government action.

Contrary to Professor Thelen, although we can find exceptions to every generalization about "progressives," most of them regarded the initiative and referendum as weapons-in-reserve in the event that they lost control of the political process. The last thing in the world that they envisioned was a continuous resort to initiative and referendum. Those were monitoring devices.

In fact, the progress on the governmental level resulted from the mobilization and participation of hundreds of thousands of people in the parties in which they had not participated before. Therefore, these were much stronger parties, according to my conception of strong parties. Of course, if we mean by strong parties strongly boss-controlled parties, and if we equate direct primaries and initiatives with weak parties, as Gerry Pomper does but I do not, then, in fact, we would assess them differently. The direct primary, as I see it, was deliberately designed to create a much stronger party. The reforms were designed to provide a basis for parties functioning as ideological instruments to represent coherent policies, rather than resources controlled by "bosses" for economic and political "profit maximization."

It became impossible, prior to 1900, to do that within the framework of the existing party organizations. The primary was intended to function as an instrument for strong parties rather than weak parties. That it was and is an inadequate device, that it does not accomplish the intended objectives, is a problem that deserves intensive, systematic analysis. Why was it so ineffective?

Why was it so incomplete? What other innovations were needed for it to work effectively?

The movement of the 1960s, as I view it, is best seen as a continuation of the "progressive"attempt to create strong, participatory parties which will, in fact, lead to effective government to "promote the General Welfare." But that claim assumes that we must deal with the issue of what we mean by strong and weak parties and how we would recognize them if we saw them.

James Sundquist

In the discussion of parties over the last few years, a simple syllogism that runs through much of the reasoning goes like this: Before the progressive reforms, parties were strong. The progressive reforms weakened parties. Strong parties are good; weak parties are bad. Therefore, we must somehow undo progressive reforms.

That is a very irrelevant line of reasoning. I have heard it today in overtones of this discussion, even in this sophisticated group. There is no way of undoing the progressive reforms. We are not going back to the old-style parties. Austin Ranney made the essential point earlier. Whether the Progressive Era was a period of strong or weak parties does not really matter. It was a period during which the party system was profoundly transformed. You can identify the old-style and the new-style postreform parties. You cannot dichotomize them quite that clearly, but you can talk about prototypes. The old-style party was Tammany Hall in its heyday or the Republican machine in Pennsylvania. The new-style party is the Democratic Farmer-Labor party of Minnesota or the participatory club movement in California or even the modern Republican party of Pennsylvania. It is quite a different thing. Nobody has ever talked seriously about getting rid of civil service and getting rid of direct primaries in order that we can go back to the smoke-filled room and the ways things were done before. That really is a profoundly irrelevant line of argument. A new ethical dimension has been brought into our whole political system that is here to stay, as Lee Benson has point out.

There is something else wrong with that syllogism. The progressive reforms did not necessarily weaken parties. They did in some cases and they did not in other cases. You can point to as many state party organizations that were strengthened by being liberated from the tight clique control that was characteristic of the old machines.

All through the North today there are Democratic parties that are by any criteria demonstrably more vital, more strong, more effective, and more productive in government than they were before. The Democratic party in Minnesota certainly is – Donald Fraser can speak to that – as well as in Michigan, Wisconsin, Maine, Vermont. There are areas where the Democratic party really did not exist until the progressive reforms occurred and set politics free from the old-style machines to which the people would not adhere, which were tightly controlled, unappealing, unattractive. The same thing can be said of the Republican party in the South. The Republican party there did not begin to move until progressive reforms and other social forces got rid of their narrow, clique-dominated organizations.

When we talk about comparing strong and weak parties, I think we need to draw a very sharp line between two types of parties. The old-style parties are not the model. Forget them. They may have been strong, but what of it? They are not coming back. The question is under what circumstances do you get strong parties of the new style, in the new political ethos of this period that grew out of the progressive movement and is not going to go away. There are a lot of models. They have not been studied. We have many studies of how Tammany Hall and the other machines performed in their heyday, so we can see them very clearly even after this lapse of time, but there has been very little done on the new parties. What distinguishes between the strong and the weak? Why did the DFL party in Minnesota flourish, win elections, and exhibit all of the normal characteristics of strength and power? Why has it declined lately? This is the fruitful line of inquire: not how do we undo the reforms and go back to where we were, but how in the new context do we devise, create, and maintain parties that can give us what we are looking for and can be strong.

Austin Ranney

Most of the people who have advocated strong parties have had quite a clear idea of what they mean by the phrase. We ought to decide if their model is what we have in mind when we talk about strong parties. A key characteristic of their model is cohesion: The party's elected public officials act together as a party, not as isolated individuals. After the party has determined its policy by some kind of intraparty discussion and majority vote, its elected officials stick to that policy. So in this model, cohesion is the sine qua non of the strong party.

A second element of this strong party model is the party leaders' ability to "vet" candidates, to look over the aspirants for the party's candidates for public office, decide which ones would be best, and then see to it that they are nominated.

A third element in the model (one which actually operates in most other party systems) is to give the national party organization the power to veto an unacceptable locally selected candidate or, in a party-list system, to put the candidates you don't like at the bottom of the list so that they will not be elected and those you do like at the top so that they will be elected.

But the essence of the model is cohesion — a party whose members vote together in support of the party's program and are responsible as a party for the results of that program. All the other values — intraparty democracy, widespread popular participation, fair representation of minority groups — are superseded by the values of cohesion and responsibility. Obviously, the reformers of the Progressive Era did not want *that* kind of strong parties.

Arthur Link

The fundamental question really boils down to one that Professor Burns raised earlier: Did the profound convulsions and changes of the Progressive Era weaken or strengthen the party system? I would answer by saying: "Yes, the structural and other changes of the Progressive Era resulted very decidedly in strengthening the party system and not weakening it."

I would point to two things: first, the Democratic party was welded into an extremely efficient and highly constructive organization, which it has not been before; second, the disruption of the Republican party in 1912 had the effect of clearing the air and settling very important questions in the GOP. Whether you like their decision or not, the decision was made in 1912, and particularly in 1916, that the Republican party would be the conservative party of the country.

Probably not until the New Deal did party discipline, cohesion, and unity exist again as it did by the end of the Progressive period. In 1920, there were two parties in existence which had high degrees of discipline and stood for definite programs and platforms. This was very much a result of the transformation of the whole political system that had come to fruition by 1920.

David Thelen

I did not expect to convert anybody here, either political scientists or historians. Obviously, you have not frustrated my expectations. However, it does seem to me, quite frankly, that the burden of proof is on those who want to defend parties as an instrument by which people can govern themselves. They do have to deal with a certain political reality — namely, that the public does not view them that way.

I feel disappointed in one sense because I had hoped the paper would allow us to build from what I think were the best features of the challenge of the democratic progressives and move ahead. I hope we can do that in our later discussions.

3

PARTY "REFORM" SINCE 1968: A CASE STUDY IN INTELLECTUAL FAILURE

Everett Carll Ladd, Jr.

Mr. [David] Mixner: Mr. Chairman, every time you let these party people have any role in the process, they'll find some way to cheat you. . . . I think most reformers now agree that you cannot allow these regular party people to have any control over anything, and still hope that you will have democracy in the parties.

Mr. [George] Mitchell: Now David, I think you're being a bit harsh here.

Mr. Mixner: There may be a few decent people, like you, George, but let me just say it again. Either you get the party people out of the process of picking delegates, or else you won't have any real democracy. . . .

It is the argument of this paper that U.S. political parties, as intermediary institutions in the democratic process, have been so seriously incapacitated as to raise problems for representative democracy. Furthermore, I argue that the

I would like to express my appreciation to Dana Suszkiw, my administrative assistant; to Linda Basilick, research associate at the Institute for Social Inquiry; and to Barry Warren, doctoral candidate in political science at the University of Connecticut, for their work in the preparation of this paper.

parties have been brought to their present condition for intellectual more than political reasons. The enfeeblement of the parties as organizations has occurred less as a necessary consequence of the pursuit of political interests than through an intellectual insensitivity to institutional requirements of representative democracy.

Something of this general failure to understand the role and requirements of parties can be seen even in the words we use to describe changes imposed upon the party system. In a thoughtful little essay, James Q. Wilson observed that "some good things and many bad things have been done in the name of reform, but the worst thing of all has been to cloak any proposal for change in the seductive disguise of that ill-used word."[1] "Reform" is the "improvement or amendment of what is wrong, corrupt, unsatisfactory." The casual labeling as "reform" of the diverse changes that have been imposed since 1968 on the structure and operations of the party system in the United States both reflects and has contributed to the unthinking acceptance of these changes as "good things" or at least as moves in the right direction. There have also been acts of pejorative labeling. Thus, strong party organization leaders are still regularly depicted as "bosses." Who among us, to prevent the improvement or amendment of what is wrong, will step forward and support the efforts of "bosses?"

The old Latin maxim nomen est numen reminds us that the way we describe something influences, as well as reflects, our understanding of it. The maxim naturally carries this corollary: To misname something is to misunderstand it. Many of the momentous changes in this century involving parties as institutions have been badly misperceived in part because of the casual and unthinking recourse to labels that praise or damn.

The misunderstanding goes far deeper than nomenclature, however. In the surge of "reform" activities since 1968, a variety of goals have been pursued that in and of themselves have merit. Their pursuit, though, has had consequences, often quite unforeseen and unintended, for the organizational health and vitality of the party system. Reform stands, unfortunately, as a classic case study of what Robert Merton described some four decades ago as the "unanticipated consequences of purposive social action."[2]

WHAT THE ARGUMENT IS AND IS NOT

So much has taken place under the general rubric of "reform" that it seems important in a paper fundamentally critical of the reform endeavor to emphasize that there is much with which I do not find fault. Reform since 1968 is no morality play, no contest of "good guys" consistently pursuing worthy goals against the forces of evil. It is, rather, a complex human endeavor in which the "bad guys" (such as they are) have often acted from exemplary motives. It is a drama characterized more by confusion than by villainy. It has encompassed, too, a number of necessary and appropriate changes. It is replete with other actions that involve collisions of interest that are important to contending groups but of little consequence to the health of the democratic process. It seems essential, in assessing the status of the political parties and the effect of reform on them, that we recognize and dismiss the many changes that have merit or are merely debatable, and that we concentrate our attention on what is now the central issue: that the net effect of reform has been to weaken the parties as institutions at precisely the time when they needed a measure of strengthening.

My criticism of the post-1968 reforms does not extend to the following. First, there was a regularization, or "modernization," of party rules and procedures. This was long overdue and its achievement salutary. I include here those measures begun at the 1968 convention and elaborated by the McGovern-Fraser Commission to provide for the timely selection of presidential nominating convention delegates. I include here, too, provisions that all state parties operate under written rules in delegate selection and that adequate public notice be given of all party meetings.

Other changes in party rules, such as the provision that delegates be apportioned among contending candidates in proportion to the candidates' strength, rather than on a "winner-take-all" basis, are more consequential than those just cited. In the context of the present paper, though, the argument over proportional representation seems of little relevance. The basic strength and vitality of parties as institutions is little affected by whether they provide for the winner-take-all or for the proportional allocation of convention delegates.

Throughout U.S. history, new groups have come forward seeking larger roles in elections. Their efforts have included the pursuit of more influence in the choice of party nominees. In the 1960s and 1970s, such groups as blacks and women have sought a larger role in presidential nominee selection, especially through the Democratic Party. The broad intent of affirmative action stipulations in the selection of delegates to the national conventions — to achieve greater representation of blacks and women — is a natural extension, then, of the historic claims of new or newly active groups. One may argue that the McGovern-Fraser Commission erred in its proposed requirement that "state parties overcome the effects of past discrimination by affirmative steps to encourage minority group participation including representation of minority groups on the national convention delegation in reasonable relationship to the group's presence in the population of the state," and in the parallel provisions with regard to women.[3] But the overall affirmative action efforts of the decade seem a reasonable response to the claims of groups that have been underrepresented in the past. In any case, whether one applauds them or objects to them, the various affirmative action requirements imposed by the national parties have surely done little, if anything, to weaken the political parties as institutions.

One can easily dispense with any serious assessment of the comparative merits of the motivations of the "regulars" and "reformers" in the reform battles since 1968. It is evident that many of the regulars sought to preserve their influence in party affairs, and that many "reformers," to enlarge their roles, promoted changes. It is evident, too, that many in both groups were genuinely motivated by concern for the health of the parties and the capacity of the parties to function effectively in the democratic process. Obviously, the reformers were more dissatisfied at the end of the 1960s and in the early 1970s and were the architects of most of the changes, but there is no basis for maintaining that one group or the other operated from motives more supportive of or antipathetic to the requirements of a healthy democracy.

The Vietnam War years were a time of extraordinary turmoil in U.S. public life. Many of the deepest divisions were within the Democratic Party. The 1968 and 1972 Democratic national conventions were bruising affairs, as proponents and opponents of U.S. involvement in Vietnam struggled to achieve their policy objectives through the making of the president. With the advantage of a little distance from the passions of the Vietnam years, we can see easily that no set of party rules or procedures could have avoided or even much mitigated major intramural struggles. The divisions were too deep. The ultimate selection of Hubert Humphrey as Democratic nominee in 1968 and of George McGovern as the party's candidate in 1972, and the outcomes of those two elections, seem essentially irrelevant to any assessment of the consequences of party reform. In *Mandate for Reform,* the McGovern-Fraser Commission argued that rules bearing upon the structure and nominating practices of the party carried responsibility for the tumult and divisiveness of the 1968 Convention. For their part, four years later, many regulars insisted that McGovern's massive electoral defeat revealed the essential error of the reform initiatives. Both views contain some measure of truth, but both are fundamentally wrong. The depth of the divisions, not the provisions of the rules, was the principal factor in the Democratic nomination contests of 1968 and 1972.

If many of the actions and arguments of party reform since 1968 no longer seem worth arguing about, one big issue remains with us. In a paper presented in 1978, in which he strongly defended the reforms of the last decade, William Crotty argued that "the basic question would be whether the party had done enough, expeditiously enough to halt the erosion of its position in society."[4] With only slight modification, I would accept that statement of the fundamental question: Have we done the right things to prevent the further erosion of the position of political parties in U.S. society and to help rebuild the parties as effective intermediary institutions? On this issue there are sharp disagreements — between Crotty and me specifically, and among those generally who attend to the status of the parties.

"REFORM" IN THE U.S. CONTEXT

It is not possible to assess the effect of changes imposed on an institution without first giving close attention to its prior condition and to the context in

which it operates. For instance, a set of actions that serve to weaken an institution might be seen as good, bad, or inconsequential, depending on whether
the institution was too strong or too weak before the actions were taken and
what functions the institution is expected to perform.

In the U.S. political context, political parties as organizations have been
relatively weak. Although the United States gave the world its first party system,
U.S. citizens have always been highly ambivalent about the institution. This
ambivalence concerning party follows in large measure from the culture's
distinctive individualism, which prompts voters to insist on their individual rights
to determine electoral outcomes, and to insist specifically on their rights, rather
than those of party leaders, to control nomination. U.S. citizens have been
uncomfortable with collective structures like parties that in any way deny the
individual's claim to more direct participation. Although the United States is
the world's oldest *representative democracy*, it has manifested a strong
attraction to a number of the assumptions and practices of *direct democracy*.
The individualism of the culture has inclined the populace to want direct participation by individual citizens in the main public affairs. During the Progressive
Era, this cultural inclination to direct democracy encouraged a variety of
actions, including some that were intended to weaken parties and that
accomplish that end. The Progressives advocated, with great success, that nominations for state and local office be controlled by voters in primaries, rather
than by party organizations. The capacity of regulars to manage party life was
decisively lessened and the theory of intraparty democracy took root to an
extent not found in any other democratic system. The direct primary remains
almost exclusively a U.S. institution.

In spite of these general inclinations of the culture, political parties long
maintained a reasonably robust organizational existence. In the post-World War
II era, however, some broad systemic changes in the U.S. social and political
system have seriously eroded many of the supports that had been holding up
the parties. One of these developments was the extraordinary increase in the
level of formal education, especially higher education. Since World War II,
U.S. citizens have become much more highly educated than ever before, have
many more sources of political information, clearly feel less dependent upon
parties as active intermediaries in the electoral process, and are thereby and
irreversibly more inclined to participate as independent nonpartisans.

The extension of governmental responsibilities through the elaboration of
the "service state" in the New Deal and post-New Deal years has further
weakened party organizations by taking a function away from them. Parties
once provided a number of social services, including aid to the needy. Nonpartisan public bureaucracies now administer such services, of course, at a vastly
higher level than the parties ever did. Although there are still some areas in the
United States where party leaders serve as fixers or "ombudsmen" for citizens
with needs or grievances regarding governmental action, the ombudsman role
has increasingly been taken over by units of public bureaucracy.

The rise of the national press has also played a part in the weakening of parties. Increasingly, the press has taken over important facets of the communication role that was once performed by party organization. As David Broder observed in a perceptive essay, the news business now serves as the principal source of information on what candidates are saying and doing. They act the part of talent scouts, conveying the judgment that some contenders are promising, while dismissing others as of no real talent. They also operate as race callers or handicappers, telling the public how the election is going. At times they function as public defenders, bent on exposing what they consider the frailties, duplicities, and sundry inadequacies of a candidate. In some instances, they even serve as assistant campaign managers, informally advising a candidate, and publicly, if discreetly, promoting the candidate's cause.[5]

At one time, most voters got their political information from the political parties, including a party press. Today, it is obvious that political parties are an essentially insignificant source of political information. As they have lost the communication function to a professional and bureaucratic press, they have lost an important role.

Most of these substantial developments that have intruded on the U.S. parties lie substantially beyond the range of our control. The United States has been, and will remain, an intensely individualistic society, and parties as intermediary institutions will always confront profound cultural biases. The communications and service functions simply cannot to any substantial degree be returned to the parties, given the structure of contemporary U.S. society. The electorates of the 1970s and 1980s will necessarily be less dependent on party leaders than were those of the 1890s and 1920s. What one might have hoped for in those areas susceptible to control was, with so much going against the parties, some modest doses of "countercyclical policy" to bolster a deteriorating but essential institution. Just the opposite has occurred, however, in the name of reform. We have been engaging since 1968 in the gratuitous weakening of an already feeble institution.

The reforms that have been made are actually not as sweeping as is sometimes suggested. The changes since 1968 are not comparable in scope to those of the Progressive Era. Specifically, there has been nothing nearly so intrinsically consequential in our period as was the general introduction of the direct primary. What makes the reform initiatives of the last decade so significant, and the overall effect of reform so unfortunate, is that they have been a push to an institution already teetering on the brink. Had political parties not already been so seriously weakened, the reforms since 1968 would not loom nearly so large as they do.

THE INTELLECTUAL PROBLEM

The McGovern-Fraser Commission maintained in *Mandate for Reform* that *internal party democracy* was the primary value to be promoted through reform, and that its achievement would make the parties more representative of the populace and thereby stronger, more competitive, and generally better able to perform their part in government. This goal of party building through internal democracy was subsequently reaffirmed broadly by the Mikulski Commission and halfheartedly by the Winograd Commission.[6] Apart from affirmative action measures, the McGovern-Fraser Commission recommended that internal party democracy be promoted by requiring that minority views be represented in all slate-making sessions. Delegates were to be chosen almost exclusively by caucuses and by convention arrangements open to all party adherents and providing proportional representation for minority candidates – or through primaries. If a state Democratic Party insisted on permitting its central committee to play a role in choosing delegates to the national convention, it was required to limit the number of delegates thus selected to not more than 10 percent of the total. Proscribed was the practice whereby "certain public or party office holders are delegates to county, state, and national conventions by virtue of their official position."

The most notable formal response to such new rules was the proliferation of presidential primaries. The Winograd Commission's report cautiously acknowledges that:

One can interpret the proliferation of primaries following 1968 as a response to the McGovern-Fraser reforms. Delegate selection processes in 1968 were criticized as closed to rank-and-file participation. The reformers emphasized the value of participation in the delegate selection process. While the McGovern-Fraser Commission was neutral on the question of primaries, many state parties felt that a primary offered the most protection against a challenge of the next convention.[7]

There had been 17 Democratic presidential primaries in 1968; the number rose to 23 in 1972 and to 30 in 1976. Whereas less than half of all delegates to the 1968 presidential convention were chosen by primaries, nearly three-fourths of the 1976 Democratic delegates (and two-thirds of the Republican delegates) were so selected. The proportion will be higher still in 1980.

Looking back on the developments where by presidential primaries became the dominant instrument for choosing convention delegates, the Winograd Commission quietly and cautiously drew this conclusion as to the result: "It is clear that state party organizations have taken more of an administrative role than a decision-making role in recent Presidential nominations."[8] This is a fair statement of the consequence of primaries. A series of measures undertaken to open and democratize and vitalize the parties, and thereby make them stronger, through inadvertence, oversight, and the unthinking pursuit of short-term group interests during the divisive struggles of the Vietnam years, have helped bring the state parties to an administrative role, rather than a decision-making role, in presidential nomination.

That the political parties could have been strengthened by stripping yet another function from them — the playing of a decision-making role in presidential nominations — seems highly unlikely. But so strong was the appeal of direct democracy notions that strikingly little attention was directed to the effect on the parties, as intermediary organizations, of the increasing recourse to primaries. As late as 1978, the Winograd Commission was still arguing that it was not unrealistic to have expected that primaries would strengthen the Democratic Party by involving more people in the acts of formal choice.[9] But it was not, of course, the Democratic Party as a collection of loyalties in the mass public that had been so gravely weakened by the various systemic changes of this century but the Democratic Party as an institution. The failure to focus attention on the organizational component of party looms large in the failure of reform.

Much of what we think of as "informed opinion" in the United States came during the 1970s to be singularly insensitive to the requirements of parties as representative institutions. The Winograd Report dismisses the remarks of McGovern-Fraser Commission member David Mixner, quoted at the beginning of this paper, as an example of an antiparty idea that was out of the mainstream of reform, but echoes of Mr. Mixner have been all around. On July 28, 1978, for example, the staid Connecticut newspaper *The Hartford Courant* editorially condemned as antidemocratic any serious effort by party leadership in the state to shape the selection of their statewide party tickets.

In the context of a far-flung primary system and feeble parties, elaborate candidate organizations have evolved. Serious contenders must create these large, personal organizations to wage the costly and far-flung campaigns that are essentially independent of parties. Once nomination is in hand, the victorious candidate is hardly about to disband the apparatus put together for the primary struggle. The candidate relies upon it, not the party, in the general election. For all the attention that has been devoted to the Committee to reelect the President, the disgraced instrument of the Nixon forces in 1972, it was in many ways a typical contemporary electoral organization. It was formed to serve the interests of one man; it placed those interests above those of the party; and its substantial resources enabled it to disregard the party in the contest for the presidency.

Although the weakening of the parties has proceeded very far indeed, we are by no means assured that an end to this progression has been reached. The proposed reform of the presidential election system by eliminating the electoral college and substituting direct election has the support of such diverse organizations as the American Bar Association, the AFL-CIO, the Chamber of Commerce, Common Cause, and the League of Women Voters. And the polls regularly show widespread, if not intense, public support for the amendment.[10] Putting aside, then, the major question of its probable effect on the character of the U.S. federal system, we can note that it would almost certainly reduce the role of the state parties further by making state boundaries irrelevant to election outcomes. Candidates would be encouraged to wage campaigns without regard to the blocs, alliances, and structures upon which state party systems are built.

Yet another proposed reform – federal funding of congressional campaigns (H.R. 1) – has strong implications for the party system. Republicans vigorously oppose H.R. 1, labeling it "the Incumbents' Protection Act of 1979." Roughly two-thirds of those incumbents, of course, are Democrats. Given the exceptional weakness of the GOP and the deterioration of two-party competition, those who are not Republican supporters might well view with some concern any proposal that offers serious prospect of further weakening the minority party. But, this question aside, federal funding of congressional campaigns, as proposed in H.R. 1, would further weaken *both* political parties as organizations. Federal funding, with dollars channeled directly to candidates, with none passing through the formal national and state party committees, would further reduce the dependency of candidates on the parties and on the interest groups that have served as the primary building blocks of party organization. This seems already to have occurred with the extraparty public funding of presidential campaigns that is in force.

ROLE OF PARTIES AS REPRESENTATIVE INSTITUTIONS

That U.S. political parties as institutions are weaker today than they have been at any time since the 1830s is not seriously disputed. Some would, of course, take issue with my assessment of how this came to pass: That, confronted with a variety of broad, systemic changes eroding the position of the parties, a number of reform objectives have been pursued that could only weaken the parties further because they strike at the institutional raison d'etre. The more that parties are pushed out of the nomination process – or, more precisely, the greater the extent to which they are reduced to an administrative and labeling role, without a decision-making function – the more general institutional deterioration they will experience. It is that simple. It is just not possible to have it both ways, to structurally incapacitate the parties and then to have them around when one wants them to perform certain functions.

The tragedy of the intellectual failure that underlies reform ventures of the past decade involves the fact that, in spite of their enfeeblement, the parties retain exclusive custody of one core democratic function – aggregating the preferences of the public for political leadership and policy choice and converting what was incoherent and diffuse to specific, responsive public decisions. Democracy has not developed any other institution that can do this. Because this function is so critical and requires organizationally robust parties – precisely what we have been giving up – we should look at it closely. It has three distinct, although closely related, components.

Representation

The potential electorate in the United States (persons of voting age) is about 150 million. It is no small task to get candidates and programs that reflect the preferences of so large and diverse a public. Put another way, effective representation is exceedingly difficult. A number of studies have documented that turnout in the primaries — now the principal means for selecting candidates at all levels in the United States — is low and skewed toward individuals of higher socioeconomic standing.[11] But even if by some stroke of fate 100 percent of a party's adherents routinely turned out in the primaries, it would be by no means be certain that representative nominees would result. Mass electorates cannot plan. They cannot readily take steps, such as the provision of "balanced tickets," through which the diversity of the population is recognized. And at another level, only parties can elaborate programs that strike a balance among competing interests and have the prospect of rallying stable coalitions behind such programs.

At times in the arguments of the last decade over the relative merits of the pre- and post-1968 procedures with regard to the representativeness of nominees, we have inappropriately restricted the issue. Representation is achieved when government effectively translates popular preferences into programs and when the public believes that the mechanisms of government are generally responsive to its wishes. When viewed in this fashion, it becomes evident that representation requires much more partisan "openness." It requires coalition building, program development, the choice of candidates who reflect popular wishes, the translation of popular wishes into programs, the ready replacement of the "ins" by the "outs" when popular majorities are dissatisfied with governmental performance, and the like. The prominence of the institutional role of parties becomes clear.

Popular Control

Parties are the necessary vehicles for achieving popular control over government and insuring the responsiveness of public institutions to popular wishes. There are so many different elective offices in a country like the United States that citizens cannot consider their votes meaningful instruments for the control of policy unless the many separate contests are linked in some understandable fashion — unless, for instance, balloting for the 435 seats of the national legislature can be seen as a competiton of one party against another, rather than the unrelated, detached competition of individuals. From the standpoint of popular control, contests within a party, or any form of diffuse factionalism, are decidedly inferior to regular interparty rivalry.

Only parties can so organize the issues that the public is able to speak effectively on them. When they provide the "conduit or sluice by which the waters of social thought and discussion are brought to the wheels of political machinery and set to turn those wheels," as Ernest Barker once put it, parties energize public opinion and extend institutional responsiveness.[12] If they make elected officials in some sense collectively, rather than individually, responsible to the electorate, parties enormously expand the level of meaningful public control over government.

U.S. citizens today in record numbers believe that governmental institutions are insufficiently responsive, that the mechanisms for translating popular wishes into public policy are failing. This sense that the engine of government is somewhat out of control lies at the heart of the loss of confidence in public decision making.[13] The problem is a complex one; it originates in a number of developments. But surely the weakness and ineffectuality of political parties as intermediary organizations contributes to the public's sense that it lacks the appropriate mechanisms for controlling government. In the absence of strong parties, the single-issue groups that have proliferated have had a field day. Individual legislators are poorly equipped to withstand the pressures of groups with intense commitments to one or another specific issue. The Committee on Political Parties of the American Political Science Association (APSA) put it well some three decades ago:

> The value of special-interest groups in a diversified society made up of countless groupings and specializations should be obvious. But organized interest groups cannot do the job of the parties. Indeed, it is only when a working formula of the public interest in its *general* character is made manifest by the parties in terms of coherent programs that the claims of interest groups can be adjusted on the basis of political responsibility. . . . It must be obvious . . . that *the whole development* [the proliferation of interest groups] *makes necessary a reinforced party system that can cope with the multiplied organized pressure.*[14]

Integration

The 1950 APSA report on political parties called for a general strengthening of parties in the United States. The stress of this report, like that of the writings of other advocates of strong parties reaching back to Woodrow Wilson, was on the role the parties play in meeting the public need "for more effective formulation of general policies and programs and for better integration of all of the far-flung activities of modern government."[15] Few of the committee's recommendations were acted upon positively. Today, the U.S. party system is less able to integrate all of the far-flung activities of modern government than was its counterpart of, say, a quarter century ago.

For one thing, at the national level the presidential and the congressional parties have drifted further apart. In contrast to the situation that prevailed as recently as 20 years ago, candidates for president now set up their own electoral organizations and go their own way with little regard for, or contact with, other sections of the party – including, surely, the congressional wing. Few members of the Democratic majority of the House and Senate, for example, had anything to do with the nomination of Jimmy Carter. Indeed, only 18 percent of Democratic Senators and 15 percent of Democratic members of the House were even voting delegates or alternates to the 1976 Democratic convention.[16] Most congressional Democrats take some satisfaction in the fact that one bearing their label is ensconced at the other end of Pennsylvania Avenue – but not all that much.

The U.S. party system has always provided, of course, for a formal separation of the executive and the legislative branches, and this in turn has made for a separation of the congressional and presidential parties quite without parallel in parliamentary systems. But in times past, the common bond of involvement in a party structure that determined presidential nominations helped to mitigate the rigid constitutional separation. That tie is gone.

Modern government is an incredibly complex instrument. It has so many different parts responsive to so many different interests that the natural centrifugal pressures are well-nigh irresistible. Party is the one acceptable counteracting, centripetal force at the national level and in the states and cities as well.

In a system built upon the constitutional separation of powers, if parties as organizational entities are not available to bridge the divisions, how can some coherence and policy direction be attained? Some look to a popular, charismatic president who is able to appeal directly to the national electorate and thus "build a fire" under the legislature. But this sort of a plebiscitary presidential solution seems generally unacceptable. Its consequences are unattractive both when it "succeeds" and when it "fails." The quiet, sustained integration that parties might provide is to be preferred over the episodic integration of a strong leader.

Parties as intermediary, representative institutions have a special role to play in the democratic process – in the complex task of representation, in providing for popular control, and in achieving some measure of integration within a centrifugally inclined government. Today, the parties are just too feeble institutionally to do a very good job in this role.

A GENERAL UNAWARENESS

The largely unthinking attack on the organizational vitality of political parties, mounted in the name of reform, has not occurred in isolation. U.S. leaders and the public seem extraordinarily inconsiderate of the requirements of representative democracy and its intermediary institutions generally. Legislatures are also under attack – one not as advanced as that on the parties, but one not to be dismissed lightly. There has been an unprecedented level of activity involving initiatives and referenda to place, for example, formal constitutional restrictions on the capacities of legislatures to provide for taxing and spending. Austin Ranney has noted that there were more referenda in 1978 than in any previous off-year election.[17] In Washington, a number of senators and congressmen have led an effort to amend the Constitution to provide for the initiative process nationally. According to Senator Hatfield's office, the proposed amendment had 56 declared Senate and House supporters in 1978. On February 5, 1979, the measure was reintroduced in the Senate with five quite diverse sponsors: Democrats DeConcini and Gravel, and Republicans Hatfield, Pressler, and Simpson. Initiative America is lobbying actively on behalf of the federal amendment and the increased use of initiatives in the states.

Such activity is a challenge to representative democracy in the name of a putatively purer direct democracy. The attack is troubling because the public simply cannot formulate the specifics of public policy, given the complexities of modern government. The public is perfectly capable of choosing between or among programs offered by parties, but cannot, save with disastrous results, function as a gigantic national legislature.

As unfortunate as these developments are, their occurrence is not at all surprising. This highly individualistic culture has long been attracted to the ideas and processes of direct democracy. In times when representative institutions are seen performing poorly, the intellectual tendency to "go around them" becomes particularly strong. Of course, the more the representative institutions are attacked and weakened, the less able they are to do their job. Over the last ten years we have been launched anew around this vicious circle.

Various groups in the late 1960s came to see the U.S. political parties as insufficiently responsive. Their response was, in the U.S. context, the natural one: Any problem with democracy requires more democracy – that is, more direct participation by individuals. Open the parties up. Provide for more mass participation in them. The parties will thereby be made stronger and U.S. democracy healthier. That representative institutions need special forms of organizational care and nurturing did not come to mind.

The development of a set of proposals to help rebuild the institutional parties lies beyond the scope of this essay. Besides, since it was an intellectual failure that brought about the problem, solutions will come if, and only if, an intellectual correction occurs. U.S. democracy cannot function effectively in the latter quarter of the twentieth century unless its core representative institutions – specifically, here, the political parties – are revived organizationally. If there is recognition of this fact, it will not be hard to find a variety of modest means that, without flying in the face of U.S. political tradition and experience, will rebuild the parties a bit and equip them better to perform their central tasks.

NOTES

1. James Q. Wilson, "Abolish 'Reform'," *The Alternative: An American Spectator* (May 1975): 9-10.

2. Robert Merton, "The Unanticipated Consequences of Purposive Social Action," *American Sociological Review* 1 (1936): 894-904.

3. McGovern-Fraser Commission, *Mandate for Reform* (Washington: Democratic National Committee, 1971).

4. William Crotty, "Building a 'Philosophy' of Party Reform" (Paper delivered at the Annual Meeting of the American Political Science Association, New York City, August 31-September 3, 1978.)

5. David S. Broder, "Political Reporters in Presidential Politics," in *Inside the System: A Washington Monthly Reader,* ed. Charles Peters and Timothy J. Adams (New York: Praeger, 1970), pp. 3-22.

6. The Commission on Delegate Selection and Party Structure, chaired by Barbara Mikulski, was set up by the 1972 Democratic convention and reported in 1974. In 1975, Democratic National Chairman Robert Strauss established a commission whose specific assignment was well-indicated by its title: The Commission on the Role and Future of Presidential Primaries. Chaired by Morley Winograd of Michigan, the commission found its assignment greatly expanded by the 1976 national convention. It became the Commission on Presidential Nomination and Party Structure and functioned as a full-fledged successor to the McGovern-Fraser and Mikulski commissions. It reported in 1978. "Reform" activity and an elaboration of the philosophy of reform were concentrated in the Democratic party and received their primary expression through the work of the three commissions just noted.

The Republican party moved haltingly in the same general direction pioneered by the Democrats. The low-profile Delegates and Organizations (DO) Committee was the Republican counterpart to the McGovern-Fraser Commission, and after the 1972 convention, the Rule 29 Committee continued the Republicans' reform efforts. The GOP adopted new procedures for delegate selection that reflect the Democrats' concern with internal democracy. Even if the Republicans had done nothing along these lines, however, they still would have felt the effects of "reform." Many of the Democrats' changes — particularly the increased use of primaries — have been written into state law and apply to both parties.

7. Winograd Commission, *Openness, Participation and Party Building: Reforms for a Stronger Democratic Party* (Washington: Democratic National Committee, 1978), p. 24.

8. Ibid.

9. Ibid., p. 25.

10. For a wide-ranging criticism of the amendment, see Aaron Wildavsky, "The Plebiscitary Presidency: Direct Election as Class Legislation," *Commonsense* (Winter 1979): 1-10.

11. See, for example, Austin Ranney, *Participation in American Presidential Nominations, 1976* (Washington, D.C.: American Enterprise Institute for Public Policy Research, 1977); James P. Lengle, "Demographic Representation in California's 1972 and 1968 Democratic Presidential Primaries," (Paper presented at the Annual Meeting of the American Political Science Association, Chicago, Illinois, September 1976; Austin Ranney, "Turnout and Representation in Presidential Primary Elections," *American Political Science Review* (March 1972); and a study conducted by Patrick Caddell and Gary Orren for the Winograd Commission and cited on pages 10-14 of *Openness, Participation and Party Building.*

12. Ernest Barker, *Reflections on Government* (New York: Oxford University Press, 1958), p. 39.

13. For more data and discussion of the public's frustration over its perceived lack of control of government and public policy, see Everett Carll Ladd, Jr., "What the Voters Really Want," *Fortune*, December 18, 1978, pp. 40-48.

14. American Political Science Association, Committee on Political Parties, *Toward a More Responsible Two-Party System* (New York: Rinehart and Company, 1950), p. 19.

15. Ibid., p. 1.

16. Winograd Commission, *Openness*, p. 18.

17. Austin Ranney, "The Year of the Referendum," *Public Opinion* (November/December 1978):26-28.

DISCUSSION OF THE LADD ESSAY

Austin Ranney

I have been reading Arthur Schlesinger's paper as well as Everett Ladd's paper, and it occurs to me that if Arthur is correct, our discussions of party reform are like giving instructions to the stewards about the arrangement of the deck chairs on the Titanic. However, I hope that what we are doing is at least standing on the bridge so that when the captain sees a large white shape in front of him we can keep him from saying, "Damn the icebergs, full speech ahead."

In that regard, it seems to me that one of the important points that Everett Ladd makes concerns the unanticipated consequences of the recent reforms. As I look back over the history of party reform since 1968 and my own not altogether praiseworthy participation in part of it, I am struck with how often the consequences have been unanticipated and unwelcome.

For example, one of the things we thought we were doing in the McGovern-Fraser Commission was restoring, strengthening, and purifying the conventions so as to hold off the demand for a national primary. But in fact, as Ladd points out, our rules precipitated much of the subsequent proliferation of presidential primaries, which Don Fraser and a great many other members of that commission, including me, did not welcome.

Let me mention a more recent major reform that has also had unanticipated consequences: the 1974 amendments to the Federal Election Campaign Act. Let's remember that these amendments were pushed by Common Cause and other decent people in order to remove the power of special interest money and to make elections clean.

I have no reason to believe that Common Cause intended either to weaken or to strengthen the parties. They cared very little about the parties one way or the other. They still don't. If the parties happened to be killed in the process of purifying the elections, that was perfectly okay with Common Cause.

In my view, the FECA amendments did not kill the parties, but they did inflict more gaping wounds out of which a good deal of party blood has been gushing since. One is the fact that almost all of the federal subsidies go to the candidates, not the parties. They get small grants to hold their conventions and get out the vote, but most of the campaigning money goes to the candidates. As a result, the parties now play almost no role in the directing of presidential campaigns, which used to be one of their major functions.

Secondly, the limits upon the contributions and the great emphasis on large numbers of small contributions make it extremely difficult for parties to raise money, for they are best at getting very large contributions from a relatively small number of donors. The more you favor small contributions, the more you advantage the causes and candidates who can stir up the passions of the moment. The reason why parties are not very good at collecting a lot of small donations, I think, is quite clear. Parties are very old hat. The Republicans and Democrats have been around forever, whereas antiabortion, cutting property taxes, Teddy Kennedy, or even Jimmy Carter are new and exciting. Such causes and candidates are the ones who can get a lot of people to contribute small amounts.

Thirdly, the expenditure limitations have greatly increased the role of television advertising and diminished other forms of campaigning. When candidates have only limited amounts of money, they are going to spend it where they think it is going to have the biggest effect. As Arthur Schlesinger correctly points out, that is television. Now television gets a much larger proportion of campaign budgets than it has ever gotten before. As a result, there are few bumper stickers, few rallies, and few campaign buttons and other campaign paraphernalia that we used to see. And by its very nature, television plays down political parties and plays up the individual, personalistic politics and campaigns of individual candidates.

Given all these unanticipated and unwelcome consequences of past reforms, perhaps the first motto of any future party reform ought to be what is said to be the first rule of the physician: First, do no harm. In the case of the parties I would say: First do no *more* harm and after that let's see if we can do a little good.

Donald Fraser

I feel compelled to respond to Everett Ladd's charge of intellectual failure by the reformers. Frequently, it has been charged that we reformers have been guilty of a bad case of "unintended consequences." I guess unintended consequences are a virus which strikes reformers, sometimes in the back. However, this phrase "intellectual failure" adds a new dimension to what took place after 1968. I would like to review exactly what did take place after 1968.

First, it must be recognized that when the reform commission Austin and I served on began its work, it did so under a convention mandate that used the words "meaningful and timely opportunity to participate." The reforms were aimed at that objective. I am delighted that the paper absolves us from condemnation for many of the things that we did, such as regularization of party rules, requiring timely selection of delegates, requiring written rules, requiring notice of meetings, and an affirmative actions requirement which has drawn a lot of criticism, but which you correctly point out has nothing to do with the functioning of the party. You even largely absolve proportional representation from anything that is bad. Therefore, having absolved us from wrongdoing by having done those things, it is not clear exactly what we did do that was wrong other than your argument that (quoting the Winograd report) in response to these largely unobjectionable reforms the state legislatures began passing presidential primary laws.

Could we have stopped the legislatures from adopting those primary laws? It would be very difficult to go back to the convention mandate requiring meaningful and timely opportunity to participate and from that derive authority to prohibit the use of presidential primaries. Whatever else one thinks about presidential primaries, they obviously do increase participation. I happen to think they are awful things, but they do open the way to participation.

I do not think it was ever contemplated by the commission that we had authority to try to stop or slow down the use of presidential primaries. I am also satisfied that a majority of the reformers, the people on the reform commission, were opposed to presidential primaries. Certainly they were opposed to the increased use of them. I gather your charge is that the intellectual failure came in that we did not anticipate how state legislators would react to these reforms. I think that charge is probably true.

Having been a state legislator myself, I have not always had a high regard for them when it comes to political party affairs. One of the things that puzzles me about those who worry that party reform has tended to put public officials out of the picture, is that the public officials are the ones who have been enacting the presidential primaries. It is also the public officials and legislators who have been enacting public financing for the presidential races.

Let me make another observation. There were many reasons why legislators wanted presidential primaries. Some states wanted the media coverage. Some states — and this is quoting Winograd — wanted to separate state from national politics. Other state parties wanted to make sure that something like the McGovern takeover of the party would never happen to them again in their caucuses. They saw the presidential primary as a way to get around that.

People also justify primaries by arguing that political parties are undemocratic. My guess is that this is what really spawned presidential primaries in the period following 1968. Indeed, there was a case to be made that in the earlier selection systems the parties were not democratic. Once that general attitude was articulated, it was inevitable, it seems to me, that people would say we should go to more presidential primaries to remedy the situation.

In 1975, the national party recognized what was happening and it was a matter of concern. Therefore, the Winograd Commission was appointed. I think it was clear that a majority of the Winograd Commission would have liked to do something about the proliferation of presidential primaries, but then President Carter was elected and a large number of members were added to the commission. The work of the commission was diverted to rewriting the rules in order to protect the incumbent.

In any event, we did not address the presidential primary problem. We need to do so, but it is going to be hard with incumbents in the White House. Incumbents in the White House range from being indifferent to political parties to being hostile to any action a national party might take that the presidents see as injurious to their own interests. It is a very unpromising picture that we face. There are a large number of party activists who have classified themselves as reformers who are concerned about this proliferation of presidential primaries.

I would like to add some comments about the financing question. I do not think the case is quite as clear as Everett Ladd has suggested.

The Democratic party has been laboring under a $9 million debt since 1968. That has been one of the big problems that has prevented the party from doing some of the things the national party ought to do. Why is there that debt? Principally, it exists because Hubert Humphrey had to go out and raise money in 1968. He could not raise enough so he had to borrow a lot. At the end of the election there was no money to repay the loans. That has been an enormous problem for the Democratic party. I do not think the debt is paid off yet, although it may be close to being paid off. One should think about that when one castigates the notion of public financing. President Carter did not leave the Democratic party or himself with a large debt. I think there are problems with the presidential financing law, but the basic idea has much to commend it.

Let me say something about H.R. 1, which proposes public financing of congressional campaigns. That is being pushed by congressional Democrats. There is no doubt about that. I was involved in some of the discussions. In both the presidential and congressional cases we need to recognize that the financing takes place after the important party function is done; namely, the selection of the candidates. If one believes that the most important role for the party is to select the candidate, which I happen to think it is, then note that the public financing comes in after that point. In some respects that makes the endorsement or nomination of a candidate through party channels even more important. I am not sure the consequences of public financing of campaigns are that bad for the parties. In the case of H.R. 1, as I recall, there is going to be a matching fund provision. Therefore, there will be continued inducement to go out and raise money, but it will encourage spreading the base for the raising of money. That is good. If you said the money had to be routed through the party, I am not sure what difference it would make. Once a candidate had survived a primary and was into a general election, whether the party or the candidate had a handle on these expenditures I suspect would make very little difference. I would like to see the parties brought into it more, but I am a little concerned that there is a generalized condemnation of these financing proposals, which I do not think is really merited.

Everett Ladd

First of all, I completely agree that we have seen in the past five to ten years a lot of different changes coming from many different directions, not from a single group. That was one of the reasons why in the paper there was not a concentration on the reform commissions per se, because the reform activity reached far beyond the work of the reform commissions. H.R. 1 and the FECA did not grow out of the commissions. Nonetheless, we are arguing about the way in which each reform impacted on the political parties. When I talk about reform as an intellectual failure, I mean the entire set of endeavors, not the role of one group or one reform alone.

Secondly, with regard to the McGovern-Fraser Commission, last week I reread their official report, *Mandate for Reform*. This document is a powerful anti-party-organization statement. I do not believe it can be read in any other fashion. It prohibits special representation at conventions of elected party officials. There was no reason for the commission to do that. There was no reason for it not to emphasize the enduring responsibilities of party organization. There was no reason for it to raise a model of party role which emphasized openness almost to the exclusion of everything else.

While I would not go as far as some people have in times past with regard to fixing blame, I still would stick to the point that the commission played a not inconsequential role in encouraging an antiparty mind set.

Donald Fraser

I would like to observe that in Minnesota the party had to make almost no change in its rules as a result of these reforms. In other words, our party's operations were consistent with the requirements laid down by the McGovern-Fraser Commission.

James Sundquist

I do not know whether I join in the general agreement that seems to be developing around this room with the views of Everett Ladd and Austin Ranney. I said I do not know because all I have learned from Mr. Ladd and Mr. Ranney in this regard is what they are against. I probably agree with what they are against, but they have not told us what they are for.

There is a general tone that we want to go back to the prereform period. Yesterday, we were talking about going back to the nineteenth century and adopting as our model the party organizations that were formed then and carried over to the twentieth century and still existed until not long ago in places like Chicago. However, those were pathological institutions that I am not prepared to accept as my model. They were corrupt; we do not have to go into details about that. They were unresponsive. They were closed. They were clique ridden. They were anything but open to change.

If we are going to deplore participation, if we are going to deplore the movement to open up the parties and let more people into decision making and widen the organizations, then we have to be in favor of swinging back to some extent in the other direction toward closing our parties again. We all remember the 1952 Republican contest and the caucuses that were held in telephone booths. There is in party organizations a natural tendency, it seems to me, to shrink and become restrictive unless they are forced to open up.

The reform movements that we have been deploring the last two days came about for very good reasons. As a matter of fact, Mr. Ladd said in his paper that one basic difficulty was that the people became educated. That is something of a giveaway. They did get onto these parties and decided they did not like what they saw.

I do not know what the model is that Austin and Everett have in mind. They did not tell us. Maybe they have written it elsewhere, but I have not come across it. However, from many of the things they have said and written, it seems to me they are thinking in terms of this very closely controlled, tightly dominated, what we used to call "boss-ridden," kind of machine. When we talk about some organization vetting candidates and doing so in such a way that it would emerge with a balanced ticket, that has to be a tightly controlled thing. You do not get a balanced ticket through a widely participatory process unless you are very lucky. Somebody has to be able to call the shots and say: "This guy goes on the ticket and this guy does not. This woman goes on and that one does not."

They mention that the party organization will set the program. Actually, our party organizations have never done that. The nearest thing to it, apart from the every-fourth-year platform exercises (which to some extent is influential, but does not carry on between elections), has been the state legislative caucuses where the party boss passes the word that says: "The deal is cooked. This is the way you fellows vote." Then they go out on the floor of the legislature and vote accordingly. We all know how those deals are cooked. A lot of money changes hands. Responsibility is not in the elected officials. It is somewhere else. The people who are accountable to the electorate are taking orders from some shadowy figures behind the scenes. Decisions are made, to use the old symbol, in smoke-filled rooms.

I do not think it is sufficient to say that we are against these new participatory trends without saying what we are for. Austin, I do not think it is enough to say "do no harm" without saying what kind of good we are purporting to do, to criticize other people's remedies without proposing the remedies of our own.

Gerald Pomper

I want to speak about a different kind of intellectual failure, and I do not mean Everett's paper. I agree with everything in Everett's paper and I have even written things very similar to what he said. The similarity actually makes me suspicious there may be an intellectual consensus, at least among some political scientists, that ought to be questioned.

Take the discussions of the latent functions of reform. We sometimes forget the manifest function. If you think about it, reform efforts have succeeded in most of their manifest intentions. Rather than considering them failures, we ought to consider them successes in many ways.

The McGovern-Fraser Commission wanted to do a number of things, and did most of them that it explicitly wanted to do. It wanted to regulate party nominations. It wanted to bring new groups into the delegate selection process. It did that.

Some people indeed *did* want to harm parties. There has been a certain knowledge on the part of reformers that Michels* was right, that whoever says organization says oligarchy. Not wanting oligarchy, the reformers did not want organizations, either. They deliberately tried to weaken parties. David Mixner, whom you quote, is very explicit about it. However, I think the sentiment is more prevalent than just one person. Some of these charges were not mistakes; they were successful accomplishments of prior intentions.

We can reach the same conclusion about the presidential finance laws. The manifest intention there was accomplished. It was to limit the amount of spending. It was to cut out very large special interest contributions. The law's advocates got what they wanted. If that harmed parties, that did not bother many people. Again, I think it was some people's intentions.

But there are more basic causes. The mass media are a critical element here. It is significant that the impact of the direct primary on state party organization really does not seem to show up until the advent of television. Even though we had 40 or 50 years of direct primaries before then, one could still talk about relatively strong parties. I even remember some discussion of how the primary system was unimportant, that reform was unimportant, because state parties controlled the nominations anyway. Primaries were criticized not because they destroyed the party but because they were a waste of time and money.

I have one final comment on institutions. A number of us had a discussion last night on direct election of the president and the abolition of the electoral

---

*Robert Michels, *Political Parties: A Sociological Study of the Oligarchical Tendencies of Modern Democracy,* trans. Eden Paul and Cedar Paul (London: Jerrold and Sons, 1915). Michels was a Swiss-Italian who set forth the idea of "Iron Law of Oligarchy" – the generalization that however democratic their forms may be, all organizations, including political parties, are necessarily and inevitably controlled by small oligarchies.

college. What was striking about that conversation was that a group of four people, all of whom were for stronger parties, were in complete disagreement on whether direct election would foster stronger parties or complete the end of the parties. That suggests an intellectual failure: If we do not know, after having discussed it for 200 years, what effects direct election of the president would have on parties, we simply have not thought the issue through or do not have the research methods to answer those questions.

William Keefe

I want to return to the question of what can be done to help the parties. My notion is that public officials — and Don Fraser has already spoken to this point a bit — bear a strong responsibility for trying to keep parties afloat. They can do this through public policy. They can do it two ways. They can resist all proposals for transforming the political system that would further devitalize the parties. Those would include the proposal for a national, one-day, single-shot primary, which would eliminate altogether any role for the parties in the presidential nominating process. They can also resist the national initiative. They can resist the abolition of the electoral college and the substitution for it of the direct election of the president.

Second, when legislation is proposed that bears on the electoral system, such as public funding of congressional campaigns, they can support provisions which would recognize the importance of political parties to the polity and which would strengthen them.

In short, I think public officials bear a peculiar responsibility for discovering ways to strengthen the parties. They bear this peculiar responsibility because, first, they are in the best position to effect change and, second, they are the ones who use the party label. They owe the party something in return.

Kay Lawson

I disagree with Bill Keefe's comments that we should look to public officials. We might like to do so, but I do not think we would get very far if we expect persons who have learned to operate without party to strengthen party. We have to go back to the parties again and suggest that there are some structures that need to be provided in order to accommodate this new participatory impulse which we hope they have begun to stimulate.

Here I suggest we have to go back to what we have always said parties are all about. We political scientists always like to say that parties are interest-aggregating institutions. When we talk about interests, we sometimes are pretty close to talking about issues. When we become upset that candidate organizations have arisen and take the place of parties, we are distressed in part because we know candidate organizations mean a focus on personalities, rather than on issues.

The next step has to be building within the parties some structures for maximizing popular participation in the discussion of issues. Something that could and should be done is for both parties to set up local meetings in their communities for the discussion of issues. Resolutions should be taken at these meetings, passed on to state-level meetings, and this process should hook up directly with the final writing of the platform.

This kind of structure, working from the base right up to the writing of the platform, is perfectly feasible. It would give the parties the opportunity to say to the people: "Look, this is what we do for you that listening to the candidate repeat his commercial ad on television ad infinitum is never going to do for you."

Linda Kerber

Yesterday, we were reflecting on the relationship between political parties and the general political culture. I would like to make a further observation. It seems to me that one of the problems that faced Jeffersonians in the early nineteenth century was the effort to link the caucus as a political mechanism to the political culture at large. They did not quite figure out how to do it. It was not figured out until the 1840s, when a mass political culture was developed.

The problem that faced party leaders was the problem of making the party not only a political mechanism but part of popular political culture so that personal identification also became partisan identification. There were people in the nineteenth century who offered as part of their self-introduction: "I am a Democrat. That is the way I think of myself." That sense of identity is what made old-fashioned July Fourth oratories so meaningful and the loss of that kind of identity with party is what makes current July Fourth oratory so unmeaningful.

If that is a sensible observation, then it seems to me one way of dealing with the McGovern-Fraser reforms is to recognize that in their own terms and in their own context they are a way of trying to make modern parties cohere with popular public political culture. In that sense, the call for participation of blacks, women, and so forth is not technical, affirmative action paperwork; rather, it is an effort to make the organization party reflect the reality of the world out there.

That is why I am troubled by our willingness to see those reforms as reforms which happened against the party. I do not think they are. I think they are an important stage in party development and in a party's realistic understanding of what its political community is.

My observation is that we have been assuming that a strong party is a good thing. In some ways it certainly is. However, I think we should always be asking at what price we are getting our strong parties.

Donald Robinson

I want to interject a question at this point to which I invite reflection. It seems to be virtually stipulated around the table that parties as organizations are weak to the point of virtual extinction. What are the consequences of this for government? Are there problems of contemporary governance which are traceable to the weakness of parties and the weakness of the party system? The other side of that question is, whether the strengthening of parties is part of the remedy for those problems?

Lee Benson

I think strong parties are absolutely indispensable to strong, effective, democratic government. The disagreement — and there is a very sharp disagreement here — is about what constitutes a strong party. As I read it, Mr. Ladd's paper is defective in its analysis of the weakness of parties and its prescriptions for strengthening them. It is simply untrue, as the paper states on page 9, that Americans have always been antagonistic to parties. Quite the contrary. As Linda Kerber suggested, Americans invented parties in the nineteenth century, particularly after 1837. Party identification was then a fundamental part of one's personal and group identity.

During the 1960s, the attacks were not upon parties per se, but upon their operation by party politicians — a radically different thing. Why were those attacks made? It seems to me that Jim Sundquist is right. The parties became pathological aberrations. As they then functioned, they distorted the normative conceptions of party, of democracy, and of a good society. All the reforms, to the extent that they worked, had manifest and latent functions. They were directed toward the problem of achieving what parties were supposed to achieve: a democratic polity, a society based on the commonwealth ideal.

In every case, the development of some attempted reform resulted from egregious political abuses. If that is granted, it follows that the reformers did not attack parties per se, but party leaders. Their objective was to make the parties democratic and participatory and represent in fact what Austin defined yesterday as "strong parties" (and I agree with him) — cohesive, principled agencies to develop policy alternatives so that government might address the needs of American society.

Judson James

There are two points I would like to make. I was surprised when nineteenth century stereotypes were invoked as a response to what Everett and Austin said. It illustrates a failure on the part of professors of history, professors of political science, and a lot of other academics that knowledge of parties is stalled back at least 50 years ago. We are still talking about political machines as though they were almost contemporary. In fact, they have largely disappeared with one major exception, and everybody brings up the exception as though it were the rule. Knowledge 50 years out of date is one of the things that makes the kind of reforms of the past 10 years possible.

Kermit Hall

I am somewhat disturbed at Professor Benson's happy description of the nineteenth century, in large measure because it puts such tremendous emphasis on voter turnout as a measure of party health. There is a great deal to suggest that traditional kinds of alliances such as friendship and kinship networks worked in the nineteenth century. That really precluded or undermined the participatory aspects of parties.

More importantly, as a resident of Charles Diggs' congressional district, I have some insight into the general problem of failure of party. What I find deficient in Professor Ladd's paper is his criticism that the McGovern-Fraser reforms have gone too far. I would argue quite the contrary: The reforms have not gone far enough.

While we think continually of the need to have parties which are programmatic, which develop policy aims and goals, we never think of parties as engines to provide some sense of ethical unity or coherence. In fact, parties are by and large derelict in the regulation of the internal membership. Those who deviate from what would be considered acceptable and ethical political practices are not punished by parties at all. That is left to Congress. I cannot say that by and large Congress has a particularly distinguished record here.

My question to Don Fraser is this: Obviously there are baneful aspects of this; I am wondering if there is somewhere in the revivification of parties a need to strengthen them by making them more responsive to the need for a sense of ethical purpose, and to extend that purpose in a way which will begin to reaggregate people, at least as I see it in the city of Detroit, who look upon politicians as charlatans at best.

David Thelen

It seems to me that this discussion should not begin with parties, but with the question of how the majority can best mobilize itself. The answer might be through parties, but it might be through something else.

I was somewhat surprised to find in the paper no evidence at all to show that parties before the McGovern-Fraser reforms governed more effectively or responsively than after. There is the assertion, but there is no evidence.

As an historian I was astounded to read this sentence on pages 16 and 17 so soon after Vietnam and the 1968 Democratic Convention: "A series of measures undertaken to open and democratize and vitalize the parties, and thereby make them stronger, through" — and here is the problem — "inadvertence and oversight and unthinking pursuit of short-term group interests during the divisive struggles of Vietnam years have helped bring the state parties to an administrative role rather than a decisionmaking role in presidential nomination." These words "inadvertence," "oversight," and "unthinking" all seem inappropriate to describe those events. Have we forgotten in such a short time how whites blocked blacks from participating in the selection of southern delegates, how Johnson-regular Democrats in nonprimary states deprived access to antiwar Democrats, and how that grim symbol of boss politics, Mayor Richard Daley, created a repressive atmosphere inside and outside the 1968 Democratic convention? In my state of Missouri, Governor Warren Hearnes told one of our delegates that he determined and announced the delegation's vote on each issue according to the needs of the Johnson-Humphrey managers. Whatever undesirable consequences, if any, may have flowed from these reforms, I think that they were a relevant and brilliant response to a real problem and certainly not an intellectual failure.

I would like to ask two questions, which I do not think you have answered. First, what is the evidence to support the idea that strong parties govern better? Faced with the performance of politicians in this period, which the McGovern-Fraser reforms were attempting to deal with, what is the evidence that they performed better? Second, and this is Mr. Sundquist's question, how are we going to bridge the gap between organization and democracy, between parties and the grass roots? I must say that when the political scientists in the room come to that question they back away. Nobody has accepted Mr. Sundquist's challenge. In the absence of anything more than academic theory to support the claims for strong parties, I can leave Williamsburg reinforced in my conviction that initiatives are a better method than parties to mobilize majority sentiment.

James Banner

We have to bear in mind that the reforms that Austin Ranney arraigned Common Cause and like groups for having perpetrated on the body politic were reforms that were brought about by the egregious, the ostensible, the paramount failure of the parties operating both within and without Congress to reform their own business and the failures of the national legislature and the presidency to meet the crying needs of the commonwealth.

It was Congress that wrote the Federal Election Campaign Act of 1974. It is not borne out by the facts that any group handed the independent-minded members of Congress of both parties a law, whether it was Common Cause, Ralph Nader, or anybody else, and said: "Here, pass this bill. You damned well better, otherwise we'll get you." That is not the way legislation is enacted. That is not what happened at that time.

It turns out that the members of Congress did not see it in their interest to pass a law that would allow greater portions of public money to go to the parties. They could have done so had they had a will. I suppose they might have done so had there been a group that was outside clamoring for such action on their part. That group did not exist.

Finally, to say that parties are weak does not require us to agree that the reforms of the McGovern-Fraser Commission or any others have gone too far. Those two propositions are not logically connected. It may well be that the reforms can go farther without weakening parties. I believe that the parties are weak for reasons that started a long time ago, that are built into the social context of the post-Second World War period. I suspect historians 25 or 50 years from now will agree that the weaknesses of party had very little to do with the so-called reforms that have been passed from 1968 on.

Frank Freidel

As the discussion has gone on this morning, I have been bothered with the feeling that we have focused upon parties more as ends in themselves than as the means to an end that we all know they are. Because my approach is an historical approach, I do keep thinking that strong parties and effective government do not necessarily go together. We sometimes have been with or without party regularity, which can be negative and stultifying, or, if it is following creative leadership, can be positive and splendid. In other words, a machine can go in both directions. It can be an instrument of evil — it can be a juggernaut — or it can be a means toward splendid ends. Parties are basically machines.

We have seen extremely rapid changes in the body politic in America as we have seen changes in other areas. Americans are a very inventive people. Now we are working upon remodeling party structures. I do not think we are going to abandon parties for a second. We are simply going through the kinds of transitions that we have gone through in past times in American history, that we most recently have gone through in the Progressive Era in turning out parties that are very different from the kinds of parties that we have seen before.

In the realm of machinery itself — and I think my analogy is a very useful one — the energy crisis is going to cause us to reinvent the automobile. In the same way to the extent to which we are dependent upon television in political campaigns, to the extent to which we are trying to bring in various groups, we are simply going to have to reinvent the political party. What comes out will be a very different sort of party, but it will still be a means to an end, which can be either good or evil. It most likely will be, as it always has been, a good bit in between.

Donald Robinson

We end up with two questions. One is what Mr. Freidel just underlined: What would a strong party look like? Those who have criticized the weakness of the parties recently have not outlined, to the satisfaction of everyone around the table, what reforms would be necessary to strengthen the parties, or what a strong party would look like. It is incumbent upon them to do so now.

The second important question we must face in the moments of discussion that remain is Mr. Thelen's: Would strong parties govern better? I think his criticisms are fair. Political scientists tend virtually to stipulate that strong parties would govern better, but in this company at least I think we ought to address that question, rather than to assume it admits to an easy answer.

Austin, will you respond to the challenge that began with Jim Sundquist, although it did not end there; namely, to outline what your model of a strong party is and how we might get to it?

Austin Ranney

We certainly are not going to go back to the old, corrupt, horrible parties that some way we had up to 1968. Jim Sundquist tells us that we got rid of those parties because people became educated, found them out, and were not having them anymore. Perhaps so. But, Jim, how do the people feel about these refurbished, modernized, clean, participatory political parties that we have today? Is there a lot more confidence in them? Have the people greatly increased their approval of and identification with the parties now that they are reformed? The evidence in the polls and in declining voter turnout is all to the contrary.

James Sundquist

As near as I can tell, they have no desire to go backward. On the whole I think they approve the reforms.

Austin Ranney

What makes you think so? The polls don't say so, and voting turnout has gone down steadily. Where is the evidence that the people approve the reforms?

Lee Benson

The reforms do not go far enough. They were steps — inadequate steps — along the way toward developing genuinely good, ethical parties that fit all those categories, those idealized qualities which Gerry Pomper talked about, qualities which we do not yet see in evidence in the way the parties actually perform. If you say, "Well, people aren't happy with them yet," neither am I. They certainly are not performing well now. The question you really have to face, Austin, is: Are they better now than they were before?

Austin Ranney

I'll be glad to face it. In my judgment they are a good deal worse than they were before 1968. They now have much less power than they had before. They perform almost none of the functions they used to perform. And the people, according to the polls, hold them in lower esteem than ever. I think they are both worse and worse off than before.

But perhaps, as Lee Benson says, that is because the post-1968 reforms have not gone far enough. I would like to hear how much further they ought to go, and in which direction. For example, we could do what some nineteenth century reformers proposed: We could pass a law making it a penitentiary offense to organize a political party. There are a few First Amendment problems there, but we could amend the Constitution to take care of that.

Or we could adopt a national primary. If what you want is maximum popular participation in presidential nominations and accurate reflection of presidential preferences you cannot beat a national primary. I guarantee that a national primary would have a minimum of 20 or 25 million people participating in the selection of the presidential nominees. That would really increase participation. It would also destroy the national conventions and make the national parties no more than labels. Is that what we want?

Donald Fraser

The parties are involved with a large number of candidates seeking office across the United States. My horseback estimate is that somewhere between 6,000 and 8,000 public offices are filled by people running on party tickets, whether it be county commissioners, state legislators, governors, congressmen, or whatever. However, much of our conversation has centered around one person: the president. We forget the 6,000 or 8,000 public offices out there that are going to be filled by election a year from next November. These candidates are very much into the party, more in some states and less in others, but they are all pretty much tied to the party label and involved in whatever party structure exists.

It is an exaggeration to assume that our process for selecting one candidate is going to control a party operation which has an ongoing responsibility to the candidates for these 6,000 or 8,000 offices, all of whom are ambitious. Increasingly, I am impressed, borrowing from the Sundquist description, with the way the parties are simply the stage on which the ambitious actors perform. So much of what happens is fueled by the fact that people are aspiring to public office all over the United States.

But let me turn to a list of things I would like to see explored as an agenda for possible action by our national party. This list does not address the larger question of whether we should move toward the British model or the Mayor Daley-type party. The list includes specific, tangible changes which I think are worthy of consideration.

First, with respect to presidential primaries — and I assume around this room there is general dislike of them as they have evolved — parties should memorialize Congress not to act on a national primary without the advice of the parties. In no event should they take action which is in derogation of the right of the national parties to manage their own affairs. The Democrats did that last time. At a recent meeting, Bill Brock indicated that perhaps the Republicans would, too. I think it would be a useful step to put both parties on record in case Congress does get some further ideas on this subject.

Second, at the national level we should pass a party rule restricting presidential primaries to electing not more than 35 or 40 percent of the delegates from any state and requiring that the rest be elected through some kind of internal party process.

Next, I would like to see the adoption of a national party rule which would in effect tell state parties that they had a right to ignore a state presidential primary if they choose to do so. If they decided, notwithstanding what the legislature had done, they wanted to stay with their caucus system, they would be free to do so. The national party clearly has that right to enact such a rule.

With respect to state primaries, which generally have been condemned here, first, I think it would be useful to proceed directly to court to challenge any requirement that conventions be held after state primaries. That clearly is a violation of First Amendment rights. A court should throw it out quite quickly.

Secondly, we ought to explore extending the Virginia law, which allows state parties to decide whether they want to go through a state primary or not. It is a way of backing off of the mandatory requirement in force in almost all states that party candidates be selected by state primaries.

Third, I think we should go to court to get a determination that those primaries are unconstitutional which impose on a party a procedure which permits voters from other parties to participate in the so-called crossover primaries.

Fourth, with respect to national parties themselves, and this is more on the Democratic side, we ought to get rid of the present regional structure which divides the country into four regions. The regions are so large as to be almost meaningless. I do not want to get into arguments here as to why this is important, but regional-level activity nourished by the national party can be a very important party-building level. We ought to have at least eight to twelve regions in the United States.

Fifth, I propose a party enrollment at the national level with a modest, waivable fee which would carry with it the right to vote for delegates to midterm conferences. That would give membership more meaning than simply a card to put in your wallet.

Sixth, the midterm conferences should be strengthened by much more planning and longer sessions.

Seventh, we should initiate a strong program of party education which would range from a study of the history of the party, and a study of these things about which we are talking today, through techniques for organizing campaigns and studies of contemporary issues. We ought to encourage states to set up responsive organizations to help carry on those activities.

Eighth, we should improve the quality and volume of the communications from the national party. The Republicans, by the way, are very far ahead of the Democrats on this. They are putting out some first-rate stuff. The Democratic party looks pathetic in comparison.

Ninth, I would like to see an international secretariat established to open up contacts with party movements in other countries as a way of enlarging horizons and providing some form of transcultural communication. Our understanding about the nature of the real world would be enhanced by contacts at the party level across national boundaries.

My tenth and final proposal is, for me, crucial. The national party ought to begin actively to encourage more political socialization across state party lines by party activists so that they begin to gain a national perspective and get to know one another. They would then become a pool which provides a collegial underpinning to help winnow out undesirable presidential candidates. There ought to be some 4,000 or 5,000 people across this country who have had a chance to interact with potential candidates, to see them in action, to listen to them debate, and to talk with them. This pool of people can play a key role in restoring to the state party level this intermediary role in helping to define the choice of candidates.

The more I listen to the strong-weak party argument, the more I wonder if it is a meaningful dichotomy. Take my state. People ask what happened to the Democratic Farmer-Labor party in Minnesota in 1978. We lost our top offices. Somehow, in people's heads, strong parties don't lose elections. That really does not make sense. Anyone here recognizes that when you have been in office for quite a long time you acquire liabilities which make your ability to govern and be useful to the public somewhat impaired. Ideally, we look for competitive parties, which assumes from time to time parties are going to lose office. However, if you do lose, there is a problem of keeping strong candidates willing to run. If they don't, then there is a downward spiral that begins to take place in the party, and then the party does indeed become weaker.

If the United States some time in the next six or eight years elects a really strong, vigorous, charismatic national president, it will transform our perception of the party system in this country. Our problem is how to get from here to there. How do we get that kind of leadership? At the moment, the process appears to rely too much on accident and circumstances beyond our control. We need to regain some control over it.

4

CAN THE PARTY SYSTEM BE SAVED?
Arthur M. Schlesinger Jr.

As this discussion has amply shown, the U.S. party system has been in a state of recurrent crisis. But typically these crises have been retrospective — more a matter of subsequent discovery by historians and political scientists than of acute concern at the time. The notable characteristic of the present crisis of the party system is the amount of contemporaneous comment it has generated. The abundance of comment registers a deeper foreboding — that the party system is confronting not reorganization, as in the past, but transmutation — or even extinction. Many factors are adduced to explain this contemporary crisis. I would like to offer a historian's thoughts as to what the crisis is *not* about and then as to what, in my judgment, it *is* about.

THE GOLDEN AGE THAT NEVER WAS

We read a good deal in the press that novel and untoward development — especially the breakdown of party discipline in Congress, the power of lobbies, the rise of single-issue political movements — are transforming U.S. politics in a startling and unprecedented way, crippling the presidency, and rendering the republic ungovernable. I wonder, though, whether these phenomena are all that novel and untoward.

Take Congress, for example. Columnists write weighty pieces implying that the current party fragmentation in the Senate and the House represents a terrible change from some golden age when legislators unquestioningly obeyed the edicts of the whips. But there never was such a golden age. Even Franklin Roosevelt, in the epoch of the so-called rubberstamp Congresses, had to fight for every New Deal measure after the Hundred Days and, with all his craft and popularity, was not uncommonly repudiated by Congress on cherished administration initiatives such as discretionary neutrality legislation and the Supreme Court plan.

Nor was indiscipline new in the days of FDR. It is inherent in the U.S. system. Parliamentary regimes, based on the fusion of power, require party discipline. But our system is based on the separation of power. Partly because of the constitutional structure, partly because of the size and diversity of the country, we have never had tight party discipline. We have a natural gift, as Tocqueville pointed out, for voluntary association. For all the cant of individualism, the United States has always been a nation of joiners. But we like to keep things loose. Tocqueville saw this point too. In the United States, he wrote, "parties are impatient of control and are never manageable except in moments of great public danger" – and he was visiting the United States in an age of presidential domination as overweening as in the age of FDR.

Tocqueville traced the unmanageability of U.S. parties to the dependence of the legislator on his constituents. "A representative," he wrote, "is never sure of his supporters, and, if they forsake him, he is left without a resource. . . . Thus it is natural that in democratic countries the members of political assemblies should think more of their constituents than of their party. . . . But what ought to be said to gratify constituents is not always what ought to be said in order to serve the party to which representatives profess to belong."

The observation that a legislator's loyalty runs to his constituents more than to his party remains true today; but it is obviously not a new truth. It is simply one of the conditions with which U.S. democracy has lived for many years and will doubtless live with for many more years to come. Of course, there have been times, as in the second half of the nineteenth century, when there was more party discipline in Congress than earlier or later. But was this really a golden age? In fact, the reputation of Congress was never lower than when it was most disciplined. Those were the times that led Mark Twain to write: "Reader, suppose you were an idiot. And suppose you were a member of Congress. But I repeat myself."

Under a system of separation of power, party discipline is likely to mean a preponderance of idiots following the leadership like sheep. There are fewer idiots in Congress today. My guess is that we have had in Congress in recent years a larger proportion of informed, educated, concerned, and independent-minded legislators than we have had since the early republic. This is the kind of legislator we are alleged to want. But the price we pay for independent-minded people is precisely their determination to make up their own minds. We can't have it both ways – a high-quality Congress and sheeplike discipline. The improvement in quality also explains, I would think, the increased defection rate, for there are fewer time-servers today and more people who, coming to

Congress to accomplish things, retire in frustration when they discover that they are not getting very far.

FEEBLE PRESIDENCY, STRONG LOBBIES

The same reflections apply to the question of lobbies. *Time* and *Newsweek* in the last year have recently run cover stories implying that the republic is confronted by some new and ghastly menace in the shape of private-interest groups bringing pressure on legislators. But we have had lobbies ever since we have had Congresses. And lobbies were never more powerful than in those years after the Civil War when we came as near as we ever have to the beatitude of party discipline. Those who think that lobbies are some fearful invention of the late twentieth century ought to read *The Gilded Age*, by Mark Twain and Charles Dudley Warner, or meditate the gaudy career of Sam Ward (1814-1884), the King of the Lobby. What is, if not an invention of the late twentieth century, a development raised to new levels of effectiveness, is the public-interest lobby; and this development provides a measure of countervailing activity against the admittedly untiring and effective interventions of the private-interest groups. Ralph Nader has become the modern response to Colonel Sellers and Sam Ward.

Nor are single-issue movements the horrifying novelty that columnists, contemplating the antiabortionists, the anti-gun-controllers, the ecologists, the homosexuals, and so on, suppose them to be. What, after all, was Madison writing about when he defined "a faction" as "a number of citizens . . . united and actuated by some common impulse of passion, or of interest, adverse to the rights of other citizens, or to the permanent and aggregate interests of the community"? The "mischiefs of faction" have been an abiding theme in U.S. history. Single-issue movements have flickered through the political scene from 1787 to 1979, whether devoted to the extirpation of Freemasonry, the abolition of slavery, the restriction of immigration, the issuance of greenbacks or (one of the most successful of all) the prohibition of alcoholic beverages. U.S. democracy has lived with these movements, too. When the Native American or Know-Nothing party was at its height, Horace Greeley predicted that it would "run its career rapidly, and vanish as suddenly as it appeared. It *may* last through the next presidential canvass; but hardly longer than that. . . . It would seem as devoid of the elements of persistence as an anti-cholera or an anti-potato-rot party would be." The Know-Nothings, it should be noted, had a far greater success in elections than any of the one-eyed movements of our own day have had.

From the historical perspective, columnists and other commentators would seem inordinately excited about what are, in fact, the standard conditions of U.S. politics. Yet there must be some reason for this excitement. The reason, obviously, is the greater salience these conditions appear to have today. And here is where the diagnosticians of the press get the order quite wrong. They argue that these conditions account for the feebleness of the presidency. On closer examination, I think it will appear that the feebleness of the presidency accounts for the salience of these conditions, or at least in good part. There is a more organic problem, which I will get to in a minute.

The absence of presidential leadership creates a vacuum in the center of our politics; and it is this vacuum that, in part, disorganizes Congress and that single-issue movements and lobbies rush to fill. The essential job of a president is to fill that vacuum. The vacuum exists today not for structural reasons but for personal reasons — the limitations of the person in the presidency — and for historical reasons — the limitations of the epoch. For our effective presidents have understood that politics is ultimately an educational process. They have communicated a sense of the direction in which they want to take the nation and a capacity to persuade their countrymen that this is the best direction for the nation to go. They have possessed, and had the power to convey, a vision of the future. Tocqueville again: "Governments must apply themselves to restore to men that love of the future with which religion and the state of society no longer inspire them."

Mr. Carter is a highly intelligent man, but his is the intelligence of an engineer, not of a political leader. He sees himself as general manager of a government, not as president of a republic. After two years of the Carter presidency, no one can tell the direction in which he wants to take the country. He has no discernible interest in the tasks of public education. He evidently regards speeches not as oppprtunities to be embraced but as duties to be suffered, and makes them, it would seem, almost deliberately boring. Or perhaps he simply has very little to say. Who can tell? In any event, he leaves the special interests and the zealots a fairly clear field.

In fairness, one must add that, even if he understood what the presidency is all about, he is in office at an unpropitious time for an exercise of leadership. I will only refer briefly here to the idea, which I inherited from my father, of a cyclical rhythm in U.S. politics. But it does seem plain enough that we have had in the twentieth century seasons of action, passion, reform, and affirmative government, until the country is worn out; whereupon we long for respite and enter into seasons of lull, apathy, cynicism, and negative government. So the acquiescent twenties succeeded the two activist decades at the start of the century; the acquiescent fifties, the crisis-ridden thirties and forties; the acquiescent late seventies, the turbulent sixties and early seventies. Demanding times and demanding leadership simply wear us out after a while.

Two things happen, however, during our periods of rest and recuperation. The national batteries recharge themselves, and the problems we neglect become intense and threaten to become unmanageable. Sometime in the eighties — 1987 might be a good year from the viewpoint of this project, although in other respects a trifle late — the dam will break as it broke at the turn of the century, and again in the thirties, and again in the sixties. Our blood will begin to flow;

there will arise a new passion for innovation, reform, experiment, a new conviction of political and social possibility, a new determination to redeem the promise of U.S. life. All this will mean both a new need and a new opportunity for presidential leadership. Competent presidential leadership will do something to fill the vacuum, and such chronic ailments of our history as fractious Congresses, aggressive lobbies, and single-issue pests will dwindle to their proper proportions.

THE ORGANIC PROBLEM OF THE PARTIES

Still, the political context will, I think, be different in the 1980s — significantly different from what it has ever been in the history of the republic. This brings me to the organic problem I mentioned a moment ago, and the organic problem is what I think the crisis of the party system is really about.

The source of our contemporary forebodings lie, I believe, in the electronic revolution of the late twentieth century and in the radical changes wrought by electronic technology in the political environment. Two electronic devices have had a particularly devastating effect on the traditional structure of politics: television and the computer. The traditional structure had, in effect, three tiers: the politician, the voter, and, in between, a cluster of intermediate agencies — most significantly, the party organization, but also the labor union, the trade association, the farm organizations, and the ethnic brotherhood — mediating between the politician and the voter, interceding for each on behalf of the other and providing the links that held the party system together.

The electronic innovations have seriously undermined this traditional structure. Television presents the politician directly to the voter, and the contemporary voters are more likely to make their judgments on what Walter Cronkite or John Chancellor show them than on what the local party or business or labor or farm or ethnic leader tells them. Computerized public opinion polls present the voter directly to the politician, and contemporary politicians is more likely to judge opinon by what is read in the polls than by what is told by the local party or other leader. The prime party function that A. Lawrence Lowell described as "brokerage" is becoming obsolete. As late as 1956, Sigmund Neumann had defined as a particular party duty: "to represent the connecting link between government and public opinion." The connection between party and leaders, Neumann argued, was vital to the two-way traffic of democracy; it was "the major function" of the party to keep the lines of communication open, and this task made parties "the controlling agencies of government in a representative democracy." But with the electronic revolution, the party lost its control of the lines of communication, becoming only one link among several and not necessarily the strongest one.

The party system lost control of other things too. Television has bred a new profession of adepts at electronic manipulation. Assembled in campaign management firms, the electronic specialists are taking political campaigns away from the party. Party loyalists have given way to technological mercenaries who work indifferently for one party in one state and for its opposition in the next state. In New York in 1978, an able old-school politician, Governor Carey, won reelection in a campaign notable for its absence of volunteer workers, party literature, campaign buttons, and bumper stickers. Carey delivered the campaign into the hands of David Garth, who shut out the political professionals and replaced organization by television.

As the political professionals yield ground under the electronic dispensation to the media manipulators, they find themselves simultaneously pushed back on another front, for television has also given ordinary people a heightened sense of participation in the political process. Back rooms have lost their legitimacy. Politics is no longer accepted as the private domain of the pols. One result has been the extraordinary revival of presidential primaries − a development that has removed the nomination from the control of party leaders. Matters are settled in primaries and highly participatory caucuses, and national conventions are now ceremonies of ratification. A person born in the last year that a convention took more than one ballot to nominate a presidential candidate would be 27 years old today. In modern times, the conjuring up of dark horses out of smoke-filled rooms would infuriate participants-by-television across the land.

Television, moreover, stimulates activism. Every new group knows about "photo opportunities" and schemes to get itself on camera. What Sam Lubell has called the "struggle for political visibility" is the means by which a newly demanding electorate presses its claims. This activism increasingly finds its expression outside the party system, often in the new form of group self-assertion, beginning in our time with the blacks in the civil rights movement and followed by students, women, Indians, Chicanos, homosexuals, and so on. All this has further weakened the sense of party identification and intensified the distrust of politicians and parties − a distrust that, substantiated by spectacular policy disgraces at home and abroad, has grown into overt and joyous hostility and results in what Sam Lubell has called "a war of the voters against the party system." You all know the statistics about the decline in voter turnout, the increase in ticket splitting, and the increase in the number of voters describing themselves as independents. Party loyalties, once as sacred as religious affiliations, are steadily fading away. Political billboards in our heterodox age more often conceal than emphasize the party of the candidate − a profound change from the time when Thomas B. Reed could say: "A good party is better than the best man that ever lived."

CAN THE PARTY SYSTEM BE SAVED?

I think the minor afflictions − congressional fragmentation, lobbies, and single-issue movements − can be overcome, as they have been in the past, by competent presidential leadership in a time when the nation is looking for change. But the struggle of the traditional party system to survive in an age when the political culture is turning against parties raises harder problems.

I must confess skepticism about many of the proposed remedies. The suggestion is made, for example, that party professionals be allocated a fixed proportion of seats in nominating conventions; that campaign funds should go to party organizations, rather than to individual candidates; and that other means should be sought to prop up the party organization against the depredations of electronic mercenaries on the one hand, and of citizen activists on the other. I doubt the merit of some of these proposals. Historically, I find it hard to justify the view, for example, that the interests of U.S. democracy would be better served had political funds been entrusted to party bosses rather than to issue-responsive candidates. Let us not romanticize the old days. New ideas have won access to politics through precisely those political crusaders who took the party away from the organization: TR, Wilson, FDR. The crusaders were responsive to needs and issues; the bosses to habits and boodle.

Nor do I find the larger proposals to centralize and discipline the parties more persuasive. This effort is against the grain of U.S. parties for reasons observed long before by Tocqueville, as well as against the spirit of the times. Specific structural reforms may have their uses; I do not see that the midterm convention has done great harm, but it has worked no miracles, either. For the problem is not imperfect structure; it is vanishing function. The attempt to shore up structure against loss of function is artificial and futile.

The party system is no longer effective as an agency of mass mobilization, or as an agency of candidate selection or as an agency of communication or as an agency of brokerage or as an agency of welfare and acculturation or as an expression of the political culture. It can be saved only by the restoration of function. I am not at all clear what function it can realistically perform beyond that of writing platforms and providing labels for the organization of legislatures and elections until a strong president at a propitious time acts to renew and revitalize that president's party for that president's own purposes. The serious remaining function for the party is as an instrument of presidential leadership.

We may indeed be beginning that slow, confused descent into an era of what Walter Dean Burnham has called "politics without parties" – to which Project '87 cannot seriously object, for that was, after all, the kind of politics contemplated by Washington and most of the Founding Fathers in 1787. This is surely the politics foreshadowed by independent voting, ticket splitting, running without party identification, professional campaign management, the substitution of television for organization, and the rise of personal movements of the sort attempted by Wallace in 1968 and McCarthy in 1976. Political leaders, like Chinese warlords or Iranian ayatollahs, might roam the countryside, building personal armies, conducting hostilities against some rival warlords and forming alliances with others, and, as they win elections, striving to govern through ad hoc coalitions in legislatures.

The prospect is not inviting. The crumbling away of the traditional parties would leave political power in the United States concentrated in the warlords and ayatollahs, in the interest groups that finance them, and in the executive bureaucracy. The rest of us might not have even the limited entry into and leverage on the process that the party system, for all its defects, has made possible. Without parties, our politics would grow angrier, wilder, and more irresponsible.

Still, we cannot call spirits from the vasty deep. "The sum of political life," wrote Henry Adams, "was, or should have been, the attainment of a working political system. Society needed to reach it. If moral standards broke down, and machinery stopped working, new morals and machinery of some sort had to be invented." This seems to me our problem — not to engage in artificial resuscitation of a system that has served its time but to invent the morals and machinery appropriate to the electronic age.

DISCUSSION OF THE SCHLESINGER ESSAY

Arthur Schlesinger, Jr.

One thing this paper illustrates is the divergence in approach between political scientists and historians, a divergence which, I think, has been a strong undercurrent in these discussions. I suppose the contrast between Everett Ladd's paper and mine emphasizes that divergence.

I have been trying in my own mind to define the contrast. Obviously, any definition coming from the historical side of the barricades is open to suspicions of self-interest, but, attempting to be as noninvidious as possible, I take it that the approach of the political scientists in discussing the problem of parties has become more and more that of model building. There obviously are heuristic values in model building, but it does create some problems for realistic discussion, for model building tends to remove the institution from the ebb and flow of circumstance, to abstract the party from the historical setting which contains so many influences that play upon institutions from without.

One result of this abstraction, it seems to me, it to create a kind of platonic essence of party. Though everyone (except Austin Ranney, whose candor is always refreshing and whose wit is essential to all conferences) shows a general tendency, when pressed, to deny that the model he has in mind is identical with any actual party system, nonetheless I think that underlying a lot of the discussion is a romantic myth of the party as being at some unspecified point in the past a marvelous institution that "aggregates" everything, reconciles everything, and, among other things, confronts issues. For example, a suggestion was made that emphasis on candidates leads to absorption in personalities and that emphasis on party organization leads to absorption in issues. This sort of deductive argument is something that historians, who think not in terms of models but in terms of the concrete party organizations they know about, look on with skepticism. There are many values to having party organization, but I do not think it helps the cause of those who believe in party organizations to exaggerate the virtues of parties or to suppose that the models they have in mind faithfully represent what has actually taken place in this vale of tears.

It seems to me that the best model is not some specific pattern of organization, but, rather, the natural dialectic of parties. When party organizations get too closed, you open them up; when they get too open, as many people here seem to think they are today, you can close them back. This is what has gone on throughout our history. It is better to think of that process than to get into fallacious abstractionism by investing too heavily in one or another unitary model.

So far as issues are concerned, if you look at the effective political leaders in this century, such as Theodore Roosevelt, Woodrow Wilson, or Franklin Roosevelt, they are precisely presidents who came to power *against* the party organization. Organization does not deal in issues; it deals in routines and boodle. What TR, Wilson, and FDR did was to take the party away from the organization, creating in the course of that their own organization. That is the dialectic.

Thus, one problem with model building is the romantic myth of the organization. Another is the tendency to suppose that the problems that afflict the party originate within the model and are to be solved within the model, whereas the tendency of the historian in viewing these things would be to give attention to the factors that come from outside the party system. The motto of the historian is: Exogeny Forever!

I have attempted in my paper to suggest that parties must be examined against certain exogenous factors such as the state of the presidency. Some have said in these discussions that only a strong party can overcome the tendencies of single-interest groups or only a strong party can provide the means for strong government. In point of fact, a strong president is much more likely to overcome the single-interest movements than the strong party is.

Indeed, the strong president is more likely to be a source of a strong party. The old Henry Jones Ford argument has hardly been mentioned today, but, as Ford pointed out eighty years ago, a prime function of the party is to bridge and thereby overcome the separation of powers. Everett Ladd suggested that a strong president would not need a strong party because he would have a Committee for the Re-election of the President. I think that omits the very important need the strong president has for a strong party in order to govern effectively. It seems to me that the best hope for the revival of the party lies, as I suggest in the paper, in a strong president coming in at a point in the cycle where affirmative government is required.

So I do think that the state of the presidency is much more of a factor in the health of the parties than supposed. The cyclical rhythm that the Schlesingers, at least, discern in American politics is also important for the health of the party. The vitality of the party depends very much on the intensity of interest in politics. At least in the twentieth century, this intensity has followed a cyclical rhythm.

The suggestion that all the problems of the parties are due to the intellectual failure of the McGovern-Fraser Commission can only remind me of Rostand's Chanticleer, who supposed that his crowing caused the sun to rise. The problems of the parties are very much deeper than minor inconveniences caused by any of the minor reforms proposed by the McGovern-Fraser Commission. Nor will they be remedied by reforming the reforms and revising the party rules once again. To understand the problem, you have to get to the deeper social context in which parties live and die.

Insofar as things such as congressional fragmentation or single-interest groups are afflictions of the parties that can be overcome, the sickness of the party system is not fatal. What does seem to put the future of the traditional party system in jeopardy is the deeper context created by the electronic revolution, the revolution in the means of communication of information. This revolution has divested the party of most if its remaining functions. The effort to shore up structure against the loss of function is not going to have any significant effect. I do hope we can address ourselves to the question of what serious function the party is likely to play in the years to come, instead of thinking that you can create a function by the reorganization of structure. If there is no serious function for the traditional party to play, then what we are likely to have in the future — and I borrow the phrase from Walter Dean Burnham — is politics without parties.

I might conclude by asking: What is wrong with politics without parties? After all, that is what the Founding Fathers began with.

James MacGregor Burns

I would like to respond to what I think is a yearning here that we talk about state politics as well as national politics. I would like to be quite concrete, which I have to be if I am going to do this. Hence, I will take a bit more time than I ordinarily would like to take. Also I would like to address the questions of whether we have to go back to some kind of old party system as we try to forge a new one.

I am going to be rather parochial. I would like to start off by talking a bit about the old politics as I saw it. I realize I am talking to a group that is deeply experienced in practical politics, even aside from the two members of Congress. I really should defer to them here, except you learn a lot more from defeat, as Germany found out after World War I, than you do from victory. Also, they come from two states with very rational politics, and I would like to talk about my state, where I think I had a taste of the old politics.

It was not the old politics about which we have been hearing. It was really politics in the sense that, just as Massachusetts in the nineteenth century anticipated many of the great, good changes in the twentieth century, I think Massachusetts was an early experiment in demoralized and fragmented politics.

I wish I had the eloquence to convey to you what it is like to run in a primary, as I did, in a situation such as that. For example, you can approach a local party chairman and open your mouth to ask for $25 or $50 — you would not dare to ask for more than that — and have him open his mouth first to ask you, the candidate, for a donation to his party. The whole thing is completely reversed.

Or take the effects of the long ballot. It was essentially set up by the Constitution and it is a vital aspect of the parties which has not been talked about much, but I think we all understand that. You go to a Polish picnic of 50 or 75 people. The long ballot has primaries for 12 or 15 offices — including county commissioner, state representative, district attorney, clerk of courts, probate clerk, and so on — and with two or three people running in the primaries for each of those offices, there are likely to be 40 or 50 candidates at that picnic with maybe 75 noncandidates. In other words, in the richness of democracy you have one candidate for every two people at the picnic.

The confusion of that, the bewilderment of these good people who have to be talked to and receive cards, and this bunch of candidates descending like locusts on their pastoral scene, is another memory of the kind of problem that one faces. I could give many more examples.

However, the result of this — and I think this is by far the most typical experience of primary candidates — is a fierce sense of the loneliness of the long-distance runner. There is a feeling you are doing it alone. There is no real help out there outside of your personal group.

Yet, even in that situation there was enough of a glimmer of party organization to make it somewhat manageable. You knew when you went into a community there would be a party committee. It might be only three people who are really active, and, typically, one in a small town, but there was something there. There was a chairman there with whom you could visit.

The fact that somebody from the national party, a John McCormack, does come in, the fact that you get $250, which is what I got from the national party, is something. But the main point is that this is a highly individualistic operation, and a desperate kind of thing, where I ended up with a feeling I had no obligations to anybody outside of a few people who had contributed to me not out of the party but out of my own personal organization, which had to be quite extensive in order to do that. Fortunately, the republic was spared my being elected to Congress, so I was not able to do any harm.

However, we here necessarily get away from the grime, the sweat, the blood, and the dust of these operations. It is not a matter of powerful parties. I desperately looked for a party boss in that situation, but they simply didn't exist.

I mention this as background because I think it might sharpen the point about the new politics of Massachusetts. Arthur Schlesinger has mentioned model building. We are doing some model building. I am going to mention here a plan in Massachusetts that is not spun out of my imagination but actually is coming out of the grass roots of that state. It is quite remarkable that this much has happened in a state such as Massachusetts. If it can happen there, it might happen anywhere!

I am talking about the Massachusetts Democratic Party charter convention of 1979. The antecedents of it are quite interesting and quite reassuring. I would like to think it came to a marked degree out of the kind of intellectual ferment and the kind of work that so many people involved in this issue have been doing over the years, going back to the Political Science Association's famous "Responsible Parties" report.

However, what the charter convention really came out of is the very demoralization itself. There are hundreds and hundreds of party people in Massachusetts who feel just as frustrated about the party as many of us do here today. We have no party state convention in Massachusetts, for example. There is no way that the Democrats in Massachusetts can get together for a convention. Everyone else does. The hairdressers do, the American Legion does, and so on, but not the party. It is a remarkable fact.

Out of this frustration came a series of hearings — literally hundreds of discussions and hearings across the state, sponsored by the Democratic state committee — leading to the appointment of a character commission very much after the national model.

This gets squarely to these questions: Do we have to follow the British model? Do we have to go back to the old politics? Do we have to go off into some kind of personalistic politics? Is there another way? I think there is.

First of all, the Massachusetts charter movement gets right to the question of how there can be a strong and participatory party in the federal system. That is the big difference between our system and other countries that have had effective parties. It is terribly hard to strengthen any party system under a federal system and under a checks-and-balances system.

This is nothing new, but I think it is interesting that it is being proposed in Massachusetts. The plan there is that the existing town and ward party organizations would remain. They would continue to be chosen at a rather inappropriate time; that is, in the presidential primary. That is not untypical in this country, but it is particularly marked in Massachusetts. It is quite interesting to choose party officials in a presidential primary. But that would remain.

However, underneath this present structure there would be created a caucus system. Again, this is nothing new. Indeed, the caucus goes way back in American history. The plan is that the caucus system would be set up on a completely participatory basis, at least for the registered Democrats of Massachusetts.

The caucus would be held on all occasions where crucial actions would be taken, such as choosing delegates to county, state, or national conventions. I will not go through that elaborate process, but I think you can understand it easily. Many of you are used to it. Under this system, whenever anything very important is done, as against talking about when the next picnic will be and that sort of thing, the caucus is held in the offices of the Democratic town or ward committee or perhaps city committee. They are the hosts. Under very strong affirmative action provisions they must invite all registered Democrats to take part in this meeting. That has been spelled out because we know there are many ways of getting around it.

Under this plan, there is not only full notification, but there is full *welcome*. There is a certain amount of arm twisting. There are newspaper advertisements. There are telephone calls to the local NAACP. Every effort is supposed to be made to bring registered Democrats into this meeting. All this will be monitored — how successfully, of course, is another matter.

A second aspect of this gets right to the heart of the federal system. Some people are more interested in local politics, some more interested in state, and some more interested in national. Some are interested in certain candidacies, others in other candidates. What we envisage is a series of caucus meetings that would be addressed mainly to elections held under different aspects of the federal system and different aspects of the separation of powers. Ideally, there would be an evening meeting that would be particularly concerned about the district attorney race and would be electing delegates to that kind of conference or convention. The meetings would not actually nominate candidates, because we are not going that far, but they would be designating or endorsing certain candidates. We do not pretend that we can do away with the primary system.

If one could draw out of the litearally hundreds and hundreds of people who are potentially interested in this party effort in regard to different candidacies and different levels of office, we would flexibly plan on this interest and mobilize it in a series of meetings that would take place and become institutionalized as the established meeting for particular kinds of races.

Kay Lawson has talked about meetings. Any of us who have been to party meetings know that there is nothing worse than the typical party meeting, even when you discuss policy. Nothing happens. The whole effort in Massachusetts is to relate discussion of meetings to the choosing of candidates. Your discussion of policy has a payoff in terms of a choice of people competing to be delegates, let's say, to a policy convention, a policy conference, or to an endorsing conference.

I could sum up the idea here in two words: leadership and engagement. The thing I found so lacking — and I am sure other candidates have found so lacking — in this solitary business is a sense of engagement with interested people, instead of transient cocktail party associations including the quickie handshake, the handing out of a handbill, and the quick visit to a home. The lonely crowd feeling is incredible. You are lonely, although constantly in a crowd, because you are not engaging with the true needs and wants of the people from whom you are trying to win votes. The whole primary campaign becomes a superficial, mindless operation. To have in existence people such as the kind of party cadre we hope to mobilize would make a profound difference for the nature of campaigns.

On the leadership score, the necessity to fill the greatest void in American politics today — and this gets to the heart of the party argument — is the absence of a cadre of local leaders or regional leaders. I go back to an important point that several have made about participation. What kind of participation? We had an enormous amount of participation even in my primary because it was a hard-fought primary. When you are accused of being an atheist and a communist — you are never just a communist in Massachusetts but you are also an atheist — it is a sharply drawn thing.

The mindless aspect of that, the superficial aspect of that as against a substantial number of people who are active in these cadres, is crucial for a government that is so dependent upon leadership as our system is.

At the state level, we are trying to recreate in Massachusetts a statewide convention. In nonelection years, this would be a policy convention; in election years, it would be an endorsing convention. We are borrowing from Connecticut's experience here with the challenge primary. That is where you have to get a certain amount of support in the state convention in order to run in the primary, so we become rather conventional as we get to other aspects of this effort.

One other aspect goes back to an earlier discussion. I think Don Fraser raised it earlier. That is the whole question of outreach. We are terribly parochial in Massachusetts. To the extent that we have party activities, we operate very much within certain borders. We are trying to devise ways to get Democratic activists meeting with people outside their towns and cities, which probably happens in other states. We feel that is very important.

I will conclude by saying that I am immensely impressed that a charter commission drawn not from academia but from the grass roots of a Massachusetts party could come up with a charter. It may look like a model to Arthur Schlesinger. It *is* a model. It may have the fate of the kind of model Arthur describes. But I have a feeling — and this is why I speak with some urgency today — that things have deteriorated so much in Massachusetts and we have created such a personalistic system of politics that we just cannot raise ourselves by our own bootstraps.

Arthur Schlesinger, Jr.

You say it has deteriorated, but as long as I have known anything about Massachusetts it has always been a system of personalistic politics. When was it so great? What has it deteriorated from? It has always been a collecting of warring tongs.

James MacGregor Burns

Since you have left the state it has gotten far worse!

Richard McCormick

I have three suggestions. First, I suspect a great deal could be done in terms of reviving parties, to the degree that they can be revived, if, for example, the candidates in 1980 were to be Connally and Kennedy. That might well receive a lot of latent party fervor.

Second, we have earlier tried to identify some possible structural changes. Between 1888 and 1892, about two-thirds of the states adopted the Australian ballot. Then, for the first time, it became necessary for the state to concern itself with how candidates were nominated. At that time, they were nominated essentially by privately conducted party primaries. Some states addressed the concerns that were raised about party primaries by moving to what can best be termed the regulated primary. Instead of having delegates elected by the usual cigarbox primaries in the back room of a saloon, delegates would now be elected to primaries under appropriate safeguards and through official election machinery.

I have always felt a deep sense of regret that that experiment was never fully tested. Instead, the direct primary thrust itself upon us in the early 1900s, with consequent dire effects upon parties. It may be that, in some form, we can try to restore to the parties not democracy but appropriate representative institutions through a device such as the regulated primary. This mechanism operated in several states for varying periods, roughly from 1895 on, although in most states by 1912 it had gone by the board in favor of the direct primary. In essence, the "purified" convention system was replaced by the direct primary before it had a fair trial.

One issue that we have not addressed in the course of our discussions, although I attempted at one point to insert it, is the place of political parties in our constitutional tradition. To the extent that we might agree that it was the intent of the framers to design a government that could not be controlled by majorities except under the most extraordinary circumstances, I find some of the expectations of parties — strong parties responsive to majorities — in conflict with what I understand to be the constitutional tradition of America.

In some of the remarks, I have also found, perhaps voiced most strongly and eloquently by my colleague David Thelen, a confrontation not only with the issues of parties, but a confrontation as well, from my own perspective, with the basic American constitutional tradition, which has not been majoritarian. That is appropriately a subject for argument.

Donald Robinson

I want to pick up where Mr. McCormick left us. It seems to me that there is a defect in our constitutional system, related to a defect in its underlying ideology. I want to say a word or two about that. Mr. Schlesinger, citing Walter Dean Burnham, says that we are about to emerge into an age of politics without parties, but that is not so bad because that is what the framers intended.

Arthur Schlesinger, Jr.

That remark, I might say, was slightly ironic.

Donald Robinson

Nevertheless, I am going to pick it up. The premise of our system is that there is a tendency for factions to develop where liberty permits them to do so. Yet the preservation of liberty and the achievement of justice require that factions be thwarted. In order to accomplish this purpose, we have a separation of powers, a bicameral legislature, a system that requires a great deal of time to pass anything at any level, a distribution of functions throughout the federal system, judicial review, and all the rest of it.

It is often noted, and certainly true, that parties are not factions. We do not mean by parties what Madison meant by factions. However, it should also be noted that a system which operates to thwart factions also thwarts parties.

The modern situation presents an unanticipated challenge to the constitutional system — unanticipated, that is, by Madison. To simplify the matter, the challenge was created by three bursts of partisan and presidential activity. I am speaking of Wilson's program from 1913 to 1917 or so, the New Deal in the 1930s under Roosevelt, and the Great Society in the 1960s under Johnson. As a result of these great creative periods, we now have in this country a positive state, which consumes an enlarged proportion of the gross national product. We have a state which performs numerous functions, each serving a clientele which strains to defend the piece of pie which it has gained.

The tendency of the system to inertia, which was intentional from the framer's standpoint, now operates to entrench these interests, to make the system sufficiently impervious to change that great changes come about only when a president galvanizes a partisan majority and produces them. Except in such periods, the system is relatively rigid and inflexible.

The question today is whether we can continue to stagger along, wasting energy; providing services, bounties, grants, and loans to those who need them least, while denying them to the neediest; neglecting the condition of the urban areas; letting inflation erode the resources of those on fixed incomes; and so on.

Thus, I am concerned about the fact that our political system now operates within a constitutional framework that can only harness, discipline, and direct public authority in those rare instances where a president is able to galvanize an overwhelming popular majority and take strong possession of the legislature, of the judiciary, and up and down the federal system. Can a system so rigid, normally so inflexible, so resistant to change, be acceptable and safe? Are we still rich enough and powerful enough to live with a constitutional system that deliberately and effectively is so resistant to change and adaptation?

Arthur Schlesinger, Jr.

If you look at it statistically, I wonder whether the periods of inertia or the periods of change are the normal ones. If you look at the twentieth century, the periods of inertia have been the decade of the 1920s, the decade of the 1950s, and the decade of the 1970s. That is 30 out of 70 years. I think periods of change are more normal than periods of inertia.

The second point is that you cannot deal with the periods of inertia by constitutional reform or structural change, because the periods of inertia come, in my belief, as a result of national exhaustion. Putting it in a different constitutional framework is not going to alter that. The situation is one which depends upon the build-up of energies for change until the dam breaks – a lot happens for a decade or two, and finally the people are worn out. That is not a situation which is susceptible to structural or constitutional remedy.

Otis Graham

Aren't most of the president's problems structural? For example, there is the "permanent government" which John Kennedy discovered when he arrived and which Richard Nixon discovered in the same way eight years later. There is the need for drastic reorganization of the executive branch. There is also the problem of the unplanning structure as well as the planning temperament of the national governing establishment. It has no capacity and little will to look ahead. These are only a few examples of the structural problems of the presidency. I would like to hear you comment on that.

Arthur Schlesinger, Jr.

I absolutely agree with the importance of the structural problems of the executive government and the problem of the president getting control over the government and problems created by the fact that 60 or 70 percent of the budget is committed in a mandatory budget. They require a lot of attention.

I do think that there are inherent obstacles to a president trying to turn an American political party into an instrument of quasi-dictatorial domination. I do think it is to the interest of a president to have a strong party in some sense, at least insofar as his relationship with Congress is concerned. As Henry Jones Ford pointed out, the party is the means by which you can overcome the fissure in our government created by the separation of powers. Therefore, a wise president will try to build up his party. He will also try to build it up as a means of enlisting popular support for his policies. That was generally the FDR model, if I may borrow that word from the political scientists.

I think a president who tried to build his party for objectives that do not correspond to popular needs and popular values would encounter in our loose system the kind of resistance that would doom his effort to failure. I am not very much worried about the possibility of a Huey Long trying to establish an NSDAP in the United States.

Arthur Link

Arthur, I think some kind Providence has normally been looking over this country. It is quite true we have had cycles of reform and reaction, but nearly every great national crisis in our history has produced great leadership. It has called it forward and it has come forth. Whether it comes from the inherent political genius of the American people, I do not know. I am not about to despair about the future of the republic. I think when the time for leadership comes, that leadership will be forthcoming.

I agree with you that presidential leadership is necessary and that the president is the one and only person who can speak for the nation and unify it, rally it, and educate it. However, what concerns me is what has happened to the office of the presidency since Truman. The presidency has now become so bureaucratized and so isolated that, in fact, we virtually have no presidency left. What I mean is that the staff of the presidential office now is so large that the president has to spend a great deal of his time administering his staff, rather than attending to the problems of the country.

President Wilson's problems were by no means simple. The burdens of the presidency in his day were much greater than they are now, although people do not realize that fact. I think that I could prove it. President Wilson conducted the presidency with one assistant. Franklin Roosevelt, before 1938, had two or three assistants. Even after 1938 he did not have very many. President Truman had four or five. Now we have a presidential staff of 300 or 400. I do not see how that office can operate efficiently so long as the president has to speak constantly through intermediaries. It seems to me the president is primarily responsible for running that office. I do not see how he can do so under present circumstances.

You have been a presidential advisor, Arthur. I would like to hear your own thoughts and observations.

Arthur Schlesinger, Jr.

I fully agree with that. I think you put it very well. The correct standards are those put down by FDR. He did not want any more assistants than he could deal with personally. He did not want his assistants to interpose themselves between him and the heads of the departments and the agencies. He did not want his assistants to build up staffs of their own. FDR operated during the worst depression and the worst war in our history. Atomic energy aside, he had greater burdens than any of his successors. At the height of the Second World War he had about a dozen top-level assistants in the White House.

Professor Burns

Absolutely.

Kermit Hall

It strikes me that one can find both a strong party and demagogues. One need look only at the South during the period of the 1930s to 1940s and the experience of George Wallace and the Democratic party in Alabama, which was a strong party.

The question at hand is really not a strong party but a strong party system. It is the interaction of two highly competitive parties which ought to strengthen party government generally. It strikes me that part of the problem at the moment is that in point of fact we do not have a competitive Republican party. We have too much one-party government.

In the same vein, while the initiative has problems, it does provide the opportunity to make parties more responsible. The whole initiative process is saying to party leaders: "Do your work. If you are not going to do your work, then we will turn elsewhere."

James MacGregor Burns

May I get a clarification? Are you saying that the southern parties were strong parties or have been strong parties?

Kermit Hall

No. I am saying that if you want to measure the strength of a party in the 1920s or 1930s by its ability to win elections, you would have to say that the Democratic party was very strong in the South. However, it also produced a kind of politics which many of us find odious.

James MacGregor Burns

Are you implying that the party in the South won those elections for Democrats?

Kermit Hall

No. I am saying, regarding the character of the party itself, that if you look at the winning of elections as a measure of success, you would find that the Democrats were successful.

James MacGregor Burns

This has nothing to do with something we call party organization, as it does not in Massachusetts. Democrats win a lot in Massachusetts without any particular role by the Democratic *party*.

Robert McClory

I would like to try to pull these different discussions together. Originally, we talked about the congressional caucus and its influence or impact as a party organization in promoting the presidency. Then, as Professor Cunningham's paper indicated, it shifted from the national Congress to the states where the organization then seemed to develop in connection with the election of President Monroe.

Jim Burns has talked about the party organization in Massachusetts at the state level and local levels. I think that the real strength of party organization emanates from the grass roots, from the local political organization. That is where I have participated. I have seen a great change there.

As Arthur Schlesinger indicated, Franklin Roosevelt and others fought against the party and they won. I do not doubt that Don Fraser has had that experience. That was my experience. I had to fight against the party in order to win. When I found the local organization, it was supported primarily by the taverns which were permitted to stay open after hours with the support of the sheriff. They in turn contributed to the political party. That has all been changed, so that we have a citizen group that supports through private contributions the political organization. It is a legitimate source.

While the strength of the national party comes from strong political parties at the local and the state levels, at the same time the national parties present quite a different problem. We have heard and read comments here about the president having his party and running his campaign. Of course, that is the way Richard Nixon did it. He disregarded us. We lost Senate elections all over the country. Governors lost. He ran his campaign in disregard of the others. That is not a way to build a strong political party.

As Mr. Schlesinger's paper indicates, the way the party is going to be strong is through its strong president who is going to give his spirit and his support to make his party strong. What I am concerned about is this: What does the minority party do to become strong when it has no president to lead it?

One thing we might do is to require the networks that are licensed under federal authority to provide opportunities for the minority party and the minority party leadership to maintain its party strength. I do not know whether Arthur Schlesinger has any comments on that, but either equal time, fair comments, or something like that is required by the Federal Communications Commission. I think that is an important thing for us to give concern to as we consider the national party structure and its development under a strong presidential leadership.

Arthur Schlesinger, Jr.

In the long run, I do not think the parties are going to be saved by structural proposals, but of the various proposals that are made, the one that seems to deserve more attention than it receives is precisely the one Congressman McClory mentions. That is the provision of free television time, certainly during presidential campaigns and perhaps as a matter of course. Most European democracies, for example, automatically provide free time during campaigns.

Television is the largest charge on campaign budgets now. Television stations owners make a great deal of money off the public airways. It would seem to me that, under the "public interest and necessity" clause in the Federal Communications Act the provision of free time for political parties would help justify the large profits that owners of television stations and networks receive from the airways. Among the various proposals, the provision of free television time is something that ought to be higher on the list for the Committee on Party Renewal. Would it get support in Congress?

Robert McClory

I would think so, yes. As you know, under the federal election laws, television and radio stations are required to provide the lowest rate that is available for political campaigning. We do get the advantage of that.

James MacGregor Burns

May I pick up on that quickly? I think your point is not only well taken, but should be broadened. Those of us concerned about strong parties are terribly concerned about the weakness of the opposition party during periods of a strong presidency. However, we think it is a matter of much more than this television idea, which is very good. It is somehow creating a foundation for the opposition party so that when it does not have a president in power it has a certain amount of autonomy, integrity, strength, and continuity which so often is lacking in the present opposition party national headquarters.

Austin Ranney

Like some of my fellow political scientists, I am not convinced that some inevitable historical cycle is going to save us. The greatest crisis of the republic to date, let us remember, was the breakdown in the 1850s, which resulted in the Civil War — the greatest collapse our system has seen yet. I recall that the crisis evoked such great leaders as Millard Fillmore, Franklin Pierce, John C. Fremont, and James Buchanan. From such great leaders save us!

You might say: "Yes, but then we got Abraham Lincoln." We did, but the crisis was beyond solution and Lincoln could not prevent the war — he could only win it. Are you confident that Jimmy Carter will be followed by a Franklin Roosevelt, rather than a Franklin Pierce?

However, it seems to me that Arthur's paper calls our attention to a development that may overshadow everything else we have discussed here. That is the fact that the mass media, and particularly television, have come to be the main channels through which political events are seen and, thus, by which the political reality on which we all act is created. Moreover, as Arthur points out, there is something profoundly antiparty about the manner in which TV presents reality. That is not because of a conspiracy by the broadcasters but because the very nature of TV forces it to focus on the personality, the individual, the unique, the pictorial, rather than on the groups and the slow developments that may be historically and politically more significant.

Given the fact that TV is not going to go away, and that the communication revolution is here to stay, given also the fact that TV by its very nature is an antiparty medium and that the medium has indeed become the message, is there any reason to expect political parties to revive in any way that would enable them to perform the functions they once performed?

Arthur Schlesinger, Jr.

That question worries me more than any other. That is why the problem of trying to define some legitimate and indispensable function that parties alone can serve seems to me so critical. I am unable to think of anything beyond that of providing labels so people know where they will sit in a legislative assembly, labels for the ballot, and the fraternal values (which are not inconsiderable) at national conventions so that people from various parts of the country can meet each other and adopt a common platform.

Beyond those things, I cannot think of a popular function for party in the age of television and the polls which is equivalent at all in its vitality or grip to the manifold functions that parties served in the preelectronic age.

Donald Robinson

I want to direct attention to the title of Arthur Schlesinger's paper: "Can the Party System be Saved?" I think several people in this room, on the basis of things they have said earlier, would want to reply: "Who cares? What difference does it make?" However, there are some of us who believe it does matter whether parties can be saved because we think parties are essential to democracy. I would like to see a paper written under the title: "Can Democracy be Achieved under Modern Circumstances?" Under the circumstances of a culture in which people have a sense of losing their moorings and lacking a sense of direction, can democracy be achieved?

The framers' answer to that was: Yes, it can be achieved if you keep it cool, if you keep it small, and if you make sure nothing much happens. One of the results of that strategy was the crisis that led to the Civil War, a crisis which built and built, and the system was not able to do anything very positive to come to grips with it.

It cannot act very positively today either, except under the circumstances of a presidential leader who galvanizes a party behind him. The primary function of parties that Schlesinger leaves us at the end of his paper is to organize a following for a charismatic presidential leader. That leaves a lot of us uncomfortable, because we are not satisfied with a definition of democracy that provides for a charismatic leader and a mobilized following.

In other words, democracy is something that has to be achieved by the efforts of a people. Modern circumstances are not very conducive. It is going to be terribly difficult to achieve democracy — that is, self-government by the people — under the cultural and technological circumstances in which we live.

Finally, in the paper's last sentence you speak of what we must do. You say we have to "invent the morals and machinery appropriate to the electronic age." I would modify that just a bit and say that we must invent morals and machinery required to achieve democracy in the electronic age. Even if some charismatic presidential leader were able to solve the problems that beleaguer us, that is not enough. This country was created to show how constitutional democracy could be made to work. For that — and here I rely upon much of the analysis in the paper — we need to figure out how to develop intermediate institutions between charismatic leaders and the citizens. Parties should play a role in that.

Richard Morris

My feeling is somewhat pessimistic about the future of parties when we realize what purposes parties served in the nineteenth century. Certainly on a grass roots basis they served two purposes: First, they provided goodies or took care of felt needs of the populace; second, they got out the vote. All that was chanted by the New Deal. Welfare and social security automatically put the government on a nonpartisan basis in between the political machines and the individuals. No one cares about getting a turkey on Thanksgiving Day and therefore no one votes for Tammany Hall any longer. That has a corrosive effect upon the impact of parties.

Then, too, what gets out the vote? If I see the candidates in my living room every evening at 6:30, I do not need to have someone ring my doorbell to get me to vote.

I do not see any evidence that there is going to be a decline in welfare or social security. I do not see evidence that there is going to be a decline of television in getting out the vote. Thus, two important functions that political parties served on a grass roots level are no longer needed. The attachment of the people to the parties on this basis has greatly eroded.

Arthur Schlesinger, Jr.

On Mr. Robinson's point, I tend to avoid the word "charismatic" because its implications seem to me misleading. I do not think we have charismatic leaders in a democracy. Hitler was a charismatic leader. Charismatic implies the complete subservience of the followers to a leader. I would not call FDR a charismatic leader. FDR was a negotiator, a broker, and a compromiser, using the political process to shepherd the country in the direction he thought it should move.

Donald Robinson

How about "plebiscitary presidency?" Doesn't that term describe the modern changes?

Arthur Schlesinger, Jr.

"Plebiscitary presidency" has constitutional implications. A plebiscitary president, as I understand the term, would mean the kind of president that Nixon thought he was going to be — a president who could withhold information freely from Congress, who could spend or not spend money appropriated by Congress, and who was accountable only every four years. The president must be held to the constitutional standards. That would exclude a plebiscitary president, as I would define the term.

What we should have is a strong president in the traditional sense. We have always had strong presidents within the Constitution. One of the resources an intelligent, strong president would wish to preserve would be the political party. That is the one hope, it seems to me, for the political party – a president who understands that.

James Sundquist

I am one political scientist who agrees with Arthur Schlesinger on the subject of exogeny. It seems to me parties essentially are dependent variables. The structure of the party system, as well as everything else about them, is determined by events that are for the most part beyond our control. We can manipulate the system a little bit through will, but it is very limited, as Austin and Arthur just agreed. I am for trying all we can, but the parties are going to be swept along by the force of events.

To a great extent, the McGovern-Fraser Commission was the product of exogenous forces. It went along inexorably and not much could have been done to prevent something along those lines taking place.

Therefore, we cannot will strong parties into being. We have to look to the factors outside. Arthur mentioned two exogenous factors. Those were presidential leadership and the electronic revolution. It seems to me there is a third which ought to be added to that list. That is the simple factor of events. A phrase that has not been mentioned at all in this conference is "critical elections." My reading of history is that parties have been revitalized at a time when great issues arose such as slavery, free silver, the depression, and the New Deal. The country polarized. People felt very strongly about what ought to be done. Parties formed around the poles as instruments by which the people fought the battle and decided to get things done. Because people were deeply and emotionally involved in these issues, they attached themselves to the parties, which became their instruments for changing society or for preserving it, whichever they wished to do. That is when people identified with parties. That is when the party became something like a church.

I am not sure, but I think that in those times there is greater participation. Maybe that is when the great leaders come along, too, as Arthur Link suggests, although I suspect that is more accident than the product of those events. At any rate, in those periods we move from one party system to another. The new party system starts out in a new competitive form with new vitality.

In talking about events today, we have to look at where we are in this cyclical rhythm of new party systems being formed and then decaying. The trouble now is that it has been 45 years since the last period of transition. We are still living with a system that is two generations old. The issues around which it formed have faded away. Attachments are necessarily weakened.

This gives rise to all the phenomena about which we are talking. People run as independents. Parties do not have much meaning any more. Why should people get excited about them when the fact is they do not stand for very much? The differences between them are not very sharp. So the age of a party system is an important exogenous factor, but one that is dependent on the independent variable, which is the appearance of historical events powerful enough to create a new party system. Presidential leadership is probably also a dependent variable in this context. It too tends to be the product of events.

Given that analysis, my private scenario is this: The country can get excited about issues. It can polarize. Parties can form around the poles. I am inclined to think it will happen again at some point, just as it always has happened in the past. Probably this time it will happen around the issue of the government's role in society and in the economy, which was the essential issue of the 1930s. If that happens, people again will get excited about parties, and parties again will become meaningful. People will come to think more in terms of parties than individuals, rather than the other way around.

It may be that this would not be enough to offset wholly the influence of television and other things that have developed, but it should certainly push our politics further in the direction of strong parties and party identification than we have been accustomed to in the past few years. I think we tend to concentrate too much on the present and fail to look at the present state of the parties in terms of where are we in the cycle of critical elections, the establishment of party systems, and the decay of party systems.

The answer to your question is: *We* probably cannot save the party system, but events can save it. I think events very well might.

James MacGregor Burns

I think we should not minimize at either the national or state level the capacity of the party to be a leadership recruitment agency. On the state level, I would point to the example of New York state, which kept an effective convention system for many, many decades in this century. If you look at the stream of leadership in both parties — the Lehman-Roosevelt-type leadership, Al Smith, and there are many other examples on the Democratic side, and the Hughes, Stimson, and Theodore Roosevelt-type leadership on the Republican side — I think you have an example of what an effective state convention can do.

On the national level, in another few decades we will be able to compare what the present system, which subordinates normal conventions, does in terms of effective presidential recruitment as against the historical convention system.

Going back to Congressman McClory's point, we want a party presence nationally that has weight when it does not have a president in power. It should be able to fend off a Watergate-type situation arising from a presidential campaign where the party was shoved aside, as it usually is. The imperial presidency, among other things, has simply drawn into its orbit what once were somewhat countervailing powers such as the cabinet, the vice-presidency, and, certainly, the party system. We would like to see a party that had some presence in sustaining, stabilizing, and restricting presidents who needed to be restricted, and supporting presidents who needed to be supported. Of course, the party has to make that decision. It suffers at the polls if it makes the wrong decision.

Finally, there is this whole question that is implicit in the cyclical view of history. I think that ought to be challenged here both in Arthur Schlesinger's terms and Jim Sundquist's terms. One trouble with the cyclical view is that the length of a cycle is very hard to predict. I think there will always be this pendulum shifting back and forth, but it shifts in a very erratic way. It is not a predictable thing, as Austin brought out very well.

On Jim Sundquist's point that parties are dependent variables and that events will change them: Sure, in a sense all activity is a cluster of dependent variables. However, finally and strategically we have to say to ourselves that those who do not sit around waiting for events are probably making them.